Switch

to

Holiness

12 Actions to be Your Best

Dr. Amanda Goodson

™

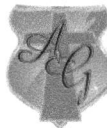
Spiritual
Quick Books

ISBN-13: 978-0615906416

ISBN-10: 0615906419

Printed in the U.S.A.

Third Edition

Switch

to

Holiness

12 Actions to be Your Best

Dr. Amanda Goodson

TM

Spiritual
Quick Books

<u>Acknowledgments</u>

Thanks to my loving husband, who loves me unconditionally and supports me continually. To my son, who I affectionately love–thank you for your energy. To my mother, sisters, and brothers – I love you!

Thanks to my friends who faithfully supported me through this process!

I especially thank Rosalyn and Noah for their great support.

TABLE OF CONTENTS

Introduction

Welcome in the mighty Name of Christ Jesus, our Lord! Are you looking to have a more intimate relationship with God on a daily basis? Looking to live a more fulfilling life separate from the norm? This book will serve as a great resource to you in getting to that place in the Lord. This book will also provide you with valuable insights into how to switch from a place of beginning to a place of richness in Christ.

People who switch to holiness make a conscious decision to be better in serving in a place of purpose. People who make the switch are convinced of the power and position that holiness carries. They understand that they have spiritual authority, and they recognize the importance and influence that the Name of Jesus Christ carries. Jesus has all authority over heaven and earth. He delegated authority to His followers and co-laborers to finish His work on earth and in the spiritual realm.

The power to carry out our all our assignments is done through the Holy Spirit. Holiness gives us the ability to be who God created us to be and to live a life far above expectations to a place of peace and authority to make disciples through the Name of Jesus. Holiness sets us apart for service and community.

Enjoy reading this inspiring book, start being your absolute best, and make the decision to: *Switch to Holiness*!

As a starting point, I would like to begin with an excerpt from my book *Spiritual Authority*.

Moses and Our Holy God:

"And the LORD spoke to Moses, saying, 'Speak to all the congregation of the children of Israel, and say to them: 'You shall be holy, for I the LORD your God am holy.'" (Leviticus 19:2)

When God spoke to Moses, He knew that Moses was a man of great integrity and had a love for living a life that honored God. God wanted the same for Israel. God sent Moses to free Israel from bondage so they could move to a place of complete promise. Being holy can bring forth great promises from God.

"You also, as living stones, are being built up a spiritual house, a holy priesthood, to offer up spiritual sacrifices acceptable to God through Jesus Christ." (1 Peter 2:5)

Believers are Living Stones with Spiritual Blessings:

Peter reminded believers that God made us all part of a royal and holy priesthood which sets us apart from all others. We serve as a spiritual house and living stones with Christ as our Cornerstone. Christ made us holy and acceptable to God through His blood. The price that Christ paid for us offered us a distinct opportunity to come before God on our own. Holiness allows the privilege of seeing God.

"Blessed be the God and Father of our Lord Jesus Christ, who has blessed us with every spiritual blessing in the heavenly places in Christ, just as He chose us in Him before the foundation of the world, that we should be holy and without blame before Him in love, having predestined us to adoption as sons by Jesus Christ to Himself, according to the good pleasure of His will, to the praise of the glory of His grace, by which He made us accepted in the Beloved." (Ephesians 1:3-6)

Holiness makes us accepted before God according to His own good pleasure. Through Jesus, we have every blessing in heavenly places.

Some people have a mental picture or image of what they believe holiness looks like. However, if we really take a look at it, holiness means you are to be set apart from sin, sanctified for God's purpose, and your life totally dedicated to Him. Jesus never expected us to be perfect, but we are commanded in 2 Corinthians 7:1 to seek perfection in holiness.

9

We see the holiness of God exhibited in His:

- Character (Psalm 22:3; John 17:11)
- Name (Isaiah 57:15; Luke 1:49)
- Words (Psalm 60:6; Jeremiah 23:9)
- Works (Psalm 145:17)
- Kingdom (Psalm 47:8; Matthew 13:41; 1 Corinthians 6:9-10); Revelation 21:27)

At the point of salvation, all believers are expected to separate themselves from all forms of false religion and make a clean break away from all sinful and old idolatrous patterns of behavior. We are to use Christ as our example and pattern our behavior after His. Although we are immediately justified at the point of salvation, the process of perfection and sanctification is an ongoing process.

Sanctification through Atonement:

We initially received sanctification through the atonement of Christ. When He died on the cross and fulfilled the will of God, we were instantly justified; we were found not guilty. At the same time, we were also 'positionally' given sanctification (see Ephesians 4:24). We took off the old sinful man and were positioned and transformed into the new. Old things passed away, and although sin and evil may still be present, as believers of Christ Jesus, we now have the ability to see them in a new light. By contrast, our efforts to achieve 'progressive' sanctification are a result of our daily walk with the Lord (see Romans 12:1-2). It's progressive because it's something we have to work on every day.

Every believer:

- Is elected and called to holiness (Romans 8:29; 1 Thessalonians 4:7)
- Must serve God in holiness (Luke 1:74-75)
- Must yield their members to God as instruments of holiness (Romans 6:13, 19)

The requirement for holiness and holy living is crucial because without it, no one can inherit the Kingdom of God (see 1 Corinthians

6:9-11). We should make a habit of practicing holiness because we are directly associated with a holy God, and it's expected that we would treat Him and His Word with respect and appreciation. We honor and glorify the Lord best by imitating Him and by being just like Him.

Some may have a hard time with the concept of holiness; perhaps because of self-condemnation or because of the condemnation of others, along with the guilt of past sin. But at the point of salvation we received God's divine grace; even though we didn't do anything to earn it. This was made possible through Jesus' substitutionary death. We are accepted in the Beloved because we are accepted in Jesus, and Jesus is automatically accepted in the Father. In other words, the Father automatically accepts Jesus, who, by His atoning blood, has accepted us. It becomes a packaged deal because we are *in* Christ.

What Happens if I Sinned?:

One may ask this question: If after I have committed a heinous crime, have been tried and convicted, and I am now serving a life sentence without the possibility of parole, how can I be accepted in the Beloved and expected to walk in holiness if I'm on permanent lock-down? It's a good question, but what's important to remember is that the seriousness of a particular past sin and the weight that it may carry as it relates to the law, is *not* a condition of being accepted in the Beloved. What is required is that we change our way of thinking. When we start thinking about the blood of Jesus and how it covers us, we will begin to get a better picture of what His atoning sacrifice really did for us. The blood of Jesus covers us, and it also covers our past sins. Once we receive Jesus as our Lord and Savior, repent, and ask for forgiveness, God doesn't see our sin any longer– He only sees the blood of His Son Jesus.

Final Introductory Remarks:

Think of how a bedspread and sheets cover a bed when it's fully made. If you pull the sheets back, you can see the truth of what's underneath; but if the bed remains made and covered by the sheets, anything that may be underneath remains hidden. That's what happened with the blood of Jesus–God doesn't see what's underneath. He doesn't see the sins of the past. All past sins have been cast into the sea of forgetfulness. God only sees the blood of His holy Son Jesus when He looks at us. And that's really good news! So switch your thinking–*Switch to Holiness*!

I trust you will enjoy reading these pages as much as I have enjoyed listening to God while developing them. I have prayed that God open your eyes to see how to be more impactful for His Kingdom through reading this Spiritual Quick Book^{TM}.

Switch to Holiness–live in your Kingdom spiritual authority, bear good fruit, and make things happen in the mighty Name of Jesus, our Lord!

1. Assess Your Domain Space

A domain is a place of influence, a realm, a thought, a sphere of action, or even a territory that you govern.[1] It is also a range of personal knowledge and responsibility that is characterized by a region that you influence or have spiritual ownership.[2]

Domain space is the space where you are currently standing, sitting, working, worshipping and living where you would influence the things around you. It is also a place where you influence others around you, or over which you have some level of authority or impact. This is a place that can be a way of thinking, it can be a range of personal knowledge, or it could be a physical territory over which you have control.

God Gave Abraham a Domain Space

"Now the LORD had said to Abram: 'Get out of your country, From your family and from your father's house, to a land that I will show you. I will make you a great nation; I will bless you and make your name great; and you shall be a blessing. I will bless those who bless you, and I will curse him who curses you.'"
(Genesis 12:1-3)

Abraham had instructions before possessing the domain (territory):

1. Get out of your country and away from your family (and the familiar).
2. Get from your father's house (and his way of thinking).
3. Go to the land (domain space) where I will show you.
4. I will make you a great nation and will bless you there.

Abram Shares His Domain Space

"Then Abram went up from Egypt, he and his wife and all that he had, and Lot with him, to the South. Abram was very rich in livestock, in silver, and in gold. And he went on his journey from the South as far as Bethel, to the place where his tent had been at the beginning, between Bethel and Ai, to the place of the altar which he had made there at first. And there Abram called on the name of the LORD. Lot also, who went with Abram, had flocks and herds and tents. Now the land was not able to support them, that they might dwell together, for their possessions were so great that they could not dwell together. And there was strife between the herdsmen of Abram's livestock and the herdsmen of Lot's livestock. The Canaanites and the Perizzites then dwelt in the land. So Abram said to Lot, 'Please let there be no strife between you and me, and between my herdsmen and your herdsmen; for we are brethren. Is not the whole land before you? Please separate from me. If you take the left, then I will go to the right; or, if you go to the right, then I will go to the left.' And Lot lifted his eyes and saw all the plain of Jordan, that it was well watered everywhere (before the LORD destroyed Sodom and Gomorrah) like the garden of the LORD, like the land of Egypt as you go toward Zoar. Then Lot chose for himself all the plain of Jordan, and Lot journeyed east. And they separated from each other. Abram dwelt in the land of Canaan, and Lot dwelt in the cities of the plain and pitched his tent even as far as Sodom. But the men of Sodom were exceedingly wicked and sinful against the LORD. And the LORD said to Abram, after Lot had separated from him: 'Lift your eyes now and look from the place where you are—northward, southward, eastward, and westward; for all the land which you see I give to you and your descendants

forever. And I will make your descendants as the dust of the earth; so that if a man could number the dust of the earth, then your descendants also could be numbered. Arise, walk in the land through its length and its width, for I give it to you.' Then Abram moved his tent, and went and dwelt by the terebinth trees of Mamre, which are in Hebron, and built an altar there to the LORD." (Genesis 13:1-18)

When Abraham became very wealthy, so did Lot–because he was moving about with Abraham. Lot was like a caddy on a golf course. When a golfer wins the championship, the caddy also earns a certain percent of the champion's prize.

The problem arose when both became very wealthy and the land couldn't support them while they stayed together. They had an abundance of cattle, flocks, and herds, and the land was too small for both of them. So, quite naturally, quarreling arose between the herdsmen of Abraham and Lot over water and grass.

Sensing this was a serious problem, Abraham knew that action was needed, and he proposed that they split. He told Lot to choose first from whatever land he wanted, trusting God for all blessings. Lot quickly responded after surveying the land below the Jordan and noticing it was very fertile. The word Jordan means 'judgment,' to 'flow down,' and 'death.'

Lot chose the land based on his external observation. The error in his decision was not valuing his spiritual life more than his material gain (see vv 10 and 13).

Lot pitched his tent near Sodom, which was a city filled with sin. He chose to be near a dead place. He didn't think about how the life near Sodom would affect him spiritually. He did not totally abandon his life of faith and actually move into Sodom right away; but he did move near it.

Lot may have begun by compromising in his heart and ignoring his conscience. But much like quicksand, once you place your feet in the mud, you soon get drawn in–until suddenly you are not able to

15

get out of it. Lot's fatal mistake was based on the gain of material wealth rather than on God's calling and His promise.

Conversely, Abraham's choice was based on trusting in God's promise. He lived a life of holiness and in accordance to the promise of God. When we live with the promise of God, we may suffer a little, but a life with God's promise is far better than a life without Him. Abraham responded by going south to Hebron, near the trees of Mamre, and there he built an altar to the Lord.

Abraham accepted God's promises and built an altar of thanksgiving and joy. The word Hebron means 'fellowship,' 'alliance,' and 'association'; and the word Mamre means 'richness,' 'strength,' and 'fatness.' He must have enjoyed rich fellowship with God there.

Joshua and the Children of Israel Were Given a Domain Space

"After the death of Moses the servant of the LORD, it came to pass that the LORD spoke to Joshua the son of Nun, Moses' assistant, saying: "Moses My servant is dead. Now therefore, arise, go over this Jordan, you and all this people, to the land which I am giving to them—the children of Israel. Every place that the sole of your foot will tread upon I have given you, as I said to Moses. From the wilderness and this Lebanon as far as the great river, the River Euphrates, all the land of the Hittites, and to the Great Sea toward the going down of the sun, shall be your territory. No man shall be able to stand before you all the days of your life; as I was with Moses, so I will be with you. I will not leave you nor forsake you. Be strong and of good courage, for to this people you shall divide as an inheritance the land which I swore to their fathers to give them. Only be strong and very courageous, that you may observe to do according to all the law which Moses My servant commanded you; do not turn from it to the right hand or to the left, that you may prosper wherever you go. This Book of the Law shall not depart from your mouth, but you shall meditate in it day and night, that you may observe to do according to all that is written in it. For then you will make your way prosperous, and then you will have good success. Have I not commanded you? Be strong and of good courage; do not be afraid, nor be dismayed, for the LORD your God is with you wherever you go." (Joshua 1:1-6)

16

Joshua was around Moses for many years and knew the promises of God and the territory (domain space) that was promised to Israel through his forefathers Abraham, Isaac and Jacob. Joshua knew, up close and personal, that having a relationship with God would reap many benefits and rewards. He also knew that disobedience and a disregard for God would cause a desert lifestyle that would last for many decades. Joshua was careful in all his actions and also knew God personally. God chose Joshua because he was fit for the job and possessed a God-given skill for strategic positioning and posturing in battle. Also, Joshua had what it took to overcome adversity in battle and would strictly adhere to God's instructions.

God gave Joshua every place that his feet would touch, just as He had promised to Moses. God gave Joshua the parameters of his domain space to acquire–from the wilderness in Lebanon as far as the great River Euphrates–all the land of the ungodly Hittites and the Great Sea toward the place that God described as 'toward the going down of the sun.' God gave distinct parameters of the land that Joshua was to possess.

Further instructions from God were for Joshua to be strong and very courageous, and that he should not look away from doing what God had instructed him. Joshua was expected to observe to do according to all that the Law of Moses commanded. In following the details of these instructions, Joshua and the people of Israel would prosper.

The book of the law was to be Joshua's everything. He was to ponder over the Word of God day and night and do all that was stated. At that point, the people would be prosperous and have great success in all they set their hands to do for the Lord.

God promised that no man would be able to stand up to Joshua all the days of his life. God backed everything Joshua did according to what He commanded him to do.

Disciples Were Promised Domain Space

"And being assembled together with them, He commanded them not to depart from Jerusalem, but to wait for the Promise of the

Father, 'which,' He said, 'you have heard from Me; for John truly baptized with water, but you shall be baptized with the Holy Spirit not many days from now.' Therefore, when they had come together, they asked Him, saying, 'Lord, will You at this time restore the kingdom to Israel?' And He said to them, 'It is not for you to know times or seasons which the Father has put in His own authority. But you shall receive power when the Holy Spirit has come upon you; and you shall be witnesses to Me in Jerusalem, and in all Judea and Samaria, and to the end of the earth.'" (Acts 1:4-8)

The disciples had been given insight into the fact that Jesus was going to grant them a domain and authority in the domain space. Jesus told them all that He was going to be leaving them and would send them some help in the form of His Spirit. Jesus sent a Counselor, Guide, Helper, Source, and Internal Agent to take care of their every need upon His departure. He brought them all together and gave them final instructions just before the cloud received Him. He told them that in a few days after He would leave that they would be baptized in a way that exceeded what John (the baptizer) had done. He told them that they would be submerged by the Holy Spirit.

He commanded that they not leave Jerusalem in order to receive this power from His Father. At that time, their domain space would be expanded and the apostles would be Jesus' witnesses in Jerusalem, Judea, Samaria and to the end of the earth. How awesome for Jesus to include us in being His witnesses today!

Jesus has Authority in ALL Domains

"Then the eleven disciples went away into Galilee, to the mountain which Jesus had appointed for them. When they saw Him, they worshiped Him; but some doubted. And Jesus came and spoke to them, saying, 'All authority has been given to Me in heaven and on earth. Go therefore and make disciples of all the nations, baptizing them in the name of the Father and of the Son and of the Holy Spirit, teaching them to observe all things that I have commanded

18

you; and lo, I am with you always, even to the end of the age.'
Amen." (Matthew 28: 16-20)

Jesus came to the disciples and let them in on a great secret–God had given Him all authority in heaven and on earth. He then let them know that they would participate in this authority. Since Jesus was going back to His Father, the disciples would continue the work that He started on earth. Their domain would include making disciples across all nations, baptizing them in the Name of the Father, and the Son and the Holy Spirit. Also, their domain (sphere of influence) would cause them to teach what Jesus had taught them throughout the ages.

God Owns it All–He is God

"He is the LORD our God; His judgments are in all the earth. He remembers His covenant forever, The word which He commanded, for a thousand generations, The covenant which He made with Abraham, And His oath to Isaac, And confirmed it to Jacob for a statute, To Israel as an everlasting covenant, Saying, 'To you I will give the land of Canaan As the allotment of your inheritance,' When they were few in number, Indeed very few, and strangers in it. ....For He remembered His holy promise, And Abraham His servant. He brought out His people with joy, His chosen ones with gladness. He gave them the lands of the Gentiles, And they inherited the labor of the nations, That they might observe His statutes And keep His laws. Praise the LORD!" (Psalm 105:7-13, 42-45)

God honors every promise that was made to us. He has allocated you a portion of the earth to manage well. What is the place where you are to influence for God? Where do you worship, work, and live that needs to be impacted for God's kingdom? Check it out and pray about it. It may be assigned to you to influence and make it a better place in which to live.

The questions that should be asked are where are you right now with God? Where has He placed you, and what has He given to you? He

19

has given all of His children the power over all the works of the enemy. God had originally given the children of Israel the authority to the Promised Land under the leadership of Moses. However, in order for them to take it, they were required to obey God's Word completely and to utterly destroy the seven (7) enemies that resided there (see Deuteronomy 7:1-6).

For us, this means that our domain space requires our total obedience to God in order for God to conquer the enemies in the earth realm. Below are seven (7) varieties of evil spirits that God will conquer.

1. Hittites/sons of terror–emotion attacks, fear and subliminal torments.
2. Girgashites/clay dwellers–analytical thinking and unbelief in what cannot be seen.
3. Amorites/mountain people–obsession with earthly fame and glory, self-exaltation.
4. Canaanites/lowlands people–addictions, carnal excess
5. Perizzites/belonging to a village–limited vision, laziness, low self-esteem.
6. Hivites/villagers–self-centered, covetous, hedonistic.
7. Jebusites/threshers–pharisaic, legalistic, enforcers of social castes.

Operating in your domain space will mean being obedient to God and operate in the fullness of His power. Below are seven revelations of His spirit:

1. Spirit of Judgment (Jeremiah 33:16)
2. Spirit of Self-sacrifice (Ezekiel 48:35)
3. Spirit of Head Authority (Exodus 15:26)
4. Spirit of Service (Genesis 22:14)
5. Spirit of Perfection (Leviticus 22:32)
6. Spirit of Dreams and Visions (Exodus 17:15)
7. Spirit of Prosperity (Judges 6:24)

Creativity is required in your domain space; and like Jabaz, one can ask for more or a larger domain space. The key is knowing and being able to boldly declare and decree (walk in with hesitation) what God's purpose is for your life. Know that your passion is directly tied to your domain space.

2. Identify Your Current Spiritual Reality

Pressing Toward the Goal

"Not that I have already attained, or am already perfected; but I press on, that I may lay hold of that for which Christ Jesus has also laid hold of me. Brethren, I do not count myself to have apprehended; but one thing I do, forgetting those things which are behind and reaching forward to those things which are ahead, I press toward the goal for the prize of the upward call of God in Christ Jesus. Therefore let us, as many as are mature, have this mind; and if in anything you think otherwise, God will reveal even this to you. Nevertheless, to the degree that we have already attained, let us walk by the same rule, let us be of the same mind."
(Philippians 3:12-16)

"Moreover, brethren, I do not want you to be unaware that all our fathers were under the cloud, all passed through the sea, all were baptized into Moses in the cloud and in the sea, all ate the same spiritual food, and all drank the same spiritual drink. For they drank of that spiritual Rock that followed them, and that Rock was Christ. But with most of them God was not well pleased, for their bodies were scattered in the wilderness. Now these things became our examples, to the intent that we should not lust after evil things as they also lusted. And do not become idolaters as were some of them. As it is written, 'The people sat down to eat and drink, and

rose up to play.' Nor let us commit sexual immorality, as some of them did, and in one day twenty-three thousand fell; nor let us tempt Christ, as some of them also tempted, and were destroyed by serpents; nor complain, as some of them also complained, and were destroyed by the destroyer. Now all these things happened to them as examples, and they were written for our admonition, upon whom the ends of the ages have come. Therefore let him who thinks he stands take heed lest he fall. No temptation has overtaken you except such as is common to man; but God is faithful, who will not allow you to be tempted beyond what you are able, but with the temptation will also make the way of escape, that you may be able to bear it." (1 Corinthians 10:1-14)

Identifying Who You Are And What You Are Purposed To Be

The first thing that should be stated is that you are not an accident. In fact, long before you were conceived in your mother's womb, God conceived you in His mind. He thought of you first and deliberately customized and prescribed every one of your characteristics.

"For you formed my inward parts; You covered me in my mother's womb. I will praise You, for I am fearfully and wonderfully made; marvelous are Your works, and that my soul knows very well. My frame was not hidden from You, when I was made in secret, and skillfully wrought in the lowest parts of the earth."
(Psalm 139:13-15)

How you view yourself will be a factor in what shapes your life. Your perspective will affect the way you spend your time and money, how you use your talents, and how you value your relationships. The most difficult thing that many struggle with is defining what they are purposed to do. Defining your purpose is very clearly stated in the Word. Accepting the assignment, however, is quite a different challenge for many.

24

"For we are His workmanship, created in Christ Jesus for good works, which God prepared beforehand that we should walk in them." (Ephesians 2:10)

We were specifically created and designed to make a difference in the earth realm. We were created, not only to add life to the earth, but also to give something back. The primary purpose for our existence in a life with the Lord is five-fold:

1. We were planned for His good pleasure (Isaiah 61:3).
2. We were formed for His family (John 15:5; Romans 12:5).
3. We were created to become like Christ (Colossians 2:7).
4. We were shaped for serving (1 Corinthians 3:5).
5. We were made for a mission (Proverbs 11:30).

Who Do Others Say You Are?

Being able to identify your current spiritual reality is knowing where you are spiritually, physically, and mentally. It requires finding your passion and discovering the talents and passions that will transform your life. Also critical is portraying a correct image to others, and asking yourself how others would perceive you in your place of employment, at home, in the community, or in church. What would others say are your strengths and weaknesses; what would you say are your strengths and weaknesses? Would you both have the same answers? You should be asking yourself the following:

- Who am I personally?
- Am I living a holy life right now?
- What needs to be adjusted?
- What is my plan and strategy for holy living?

In order to be able to answer these questions, you should have an understanding of the different temperaments or personality types that may affect your actions. Although we are not to be labeled and put into a box, these temperaments are provided for you as a guide. There are four (4) basic temperaments: Phlegmatics, Melancolics, Cholerics, and Sanguines.[1]

- <u>Phlegmatic</u>: Someone who is usually relaxed and quiet; someone who is a peacemaker in the office or church; and is always striving for a win-win for everyone; someone who may not seem to be very ambitious, but very happy to support and encourage others who are; someone unable to say no easily, and as a result, may end up working on a committee, whether they actually want to or not. These people are peacemakers and your organizational glue.

- <u>Melancholic</u>: Someone who is analytical and thoughtful; loves playing with spreadsheets, charts and projections, but may never make a decision on the spot (they have a need to think things through thoroughly); someone who will buy a car based on its fuel economy, servicing costs, and resell value, but never because of its color. These people are detail oriented.

- <u>Choleric</u>: Someone who is ambitious and leader-like; this is a take charge person whose view is the way things will probably get done; someone who doesn't take business or church rejection personally; someone who isn't interested in how exciting a project might be, but is only interested in how much money it will cost. These people are your bottom line leaders.

- <u>Sanguine</u>: Someone who is sociable and seeks pleasure; someone who will may have a messy desk and leaves projects 75% completed because of multiple distractions; makes instant decisions and communicates ideas easily; someone who is usually fashionably late to meetings, events, and parties. These people are your social organizers.

There is a myriad of personalities that make up the human race, and you may be able to identify yourself in any combination of the four basic temperaments. However, the primary concern is that we each understand that holiness is a fruit (of God's righteousness) that is not stodgy and boring; it is not aloof and unattainable. What it is, however, is a combination of many personalities, and denotes a person who readily accepts the obligations which arise from the covenant people's relationship to God. One who walks in holiness is one who has been consecrated, devoted and set apart from a common (ordinary, vulgar, and unrefined) use to a sacred (dedicated and set apart) use.

A person who is holy can also be fun-loving and spontaneous; they can be relaxed and quiet; or they can be ambitious and driven. Holiness is not limited in terms of who can possess its qualities.

The root thought regarding holiness is separation. This is a separation from all that is evil and impure, and a dedication of your whole heart and life to doing the will of God. Therefore, holiness is a willingness to yield yourself to God in a spirit of entire submission. This type of surrender must come in its entirety–it includes body, soul, life, talents, reputation–everything. The use of these things only comes when, where, and as God demands.

Nothing is impossible with God: What You Want to Achieve and The Tools to Get the Job Done

What is important to know in being able to be all and do all that God has created you to do is in remembering that God deserves your best. However, He doesn't want you to be anxious about, nor to covet or be envious over, abilities that have yet to emerge. Rather, He wants you focus on those talents specifically for your given assignments. Trying to serve God in areas out of God's divine timing is like trying to fit a square peg into a round hole. The longer you try to push to force it, or make it fit, the more frustrating and irritating it becomes; and what you produce may have limited results.

To best way to discover your best fit and know that you have the right tools for what God has intended for you is to begin at the foundation. Start by taking an assessment of your true gifts and abilities. Take a long and honest look at what you are good at, and what you are not good at. First make a list then ask other people (that you trust) for their frank opinions. Let them know you are not fishing for compliments, but you are seeking honest and candid opinions. If, for example, you believe that you would be a good leader, the easiest way to tell is by taking a look over your shoulder. If there is no one following you, then you're probably not likely to be a leader in that area just yet. As you move toward God's plan for you…your promised leadership path will emerge.

Secondly, start to ask yourself some probing questions. Some of the questions that should be asked are: Where has there been fruit in my life that can be confirmed by others? Where are the places that I have already been successful?

The key factor to note is that you will not actually know which areas you are successful in until you have begun to really serve in some capacity or other. Start out by doing some things that you have never tried before. If something does not work out for you, don't label it, or yourself, a failure; call it an opportunity or an experiment—a demonstration to examine truth.

The next thing to do is consider your personality and your heart. Carefully explore where your place of passion lies. What do you really enjoy doing most? When do you feel most alive? What are you usually doing when you lose track of time? Are you mostly introverted or extroverted? Are you a thinker or a feeler? What do you do that makes you feel the most energized—competing or cooperating?

"Have you suffered so many things in vain—if indeed it was in vain?" (Galatians 3:4)

Finally, take an examination of your life and consider the things that have shaped you (the things that you thought were both good and bad). It has been said that 'forgotten experiences are worthless.' It's not until after we have experienced something that we begin to understand how God may have intended it to be for our good. This is why it's a good idea to keep a spiritual journal.

Propelled Into Purpose

There may be times when spiritual tension will propel you into the place of purpose and spiritual reality. Often times that tension comes from the choices we make when faced with temptation.

"My brethren, count it all joy when you fall into various trials, knowing that the testing of your faith produces patience. But let patience have its perfect work, that you may be perfect and complete, lacking nothing. ... Blessed is the man who endures temptation; for when he has been approved, he will receive the crown of life which the Lord has promised to those who love Him."
(James 1:2-5, 12)

The Lord allows temptations and trials to come for the purpose of us discovering our true nature. These types of tests are to prove and increase our strength and the quality of our faith, and to demonstrate its validity. Every trial is a test of our faith and designed to strengthen us.

Consider the process of weight training. The typical weight training plan is designed to strengthen the body. An average weight training week might include intense training three times per week on alternating days with aerobics, and may look similar to the following:

Day 1: Upper body–chest/shoulders/triceps/back/biceps
Day 2: Cardiovascular Workout
Day 3: Lower body & abs–quads/hamstring/calves/abdominals
Day 4: Cardiovascular Workout
Day 5: Upper body–chest/shoulders/triceps/back/biceps
Day 6: Cardiovascular Workout
Day 7: Rest

Once all these have been mastered and the training becomes easier to get through, then the weights should become heavier and the workout more intense. The training is not designed to defeat you, but to make you stronger. The more intense the workout, the heavier the weight, the greater and stronger your muscles become, and the better able the body becomes to withstand intense weight pressure. By becoming stronger and increasing muscular endurance, you become able to perform more efficiently and avoid becoming injured.

Some of the physiological adaptations to weight training will include:

- Increased strength of tendons and ligaments
- Increased bone density and strength to resist fractures
- Improved heart rate and increased metabolism

Strength training can be seen in the spiritual realm as well. As we go through life and are faced with many challenges and temptations, choices must be made. Every obstacle and obstruction along our journey serves to create a challenge and an opportunity.

Matthew 7:13-27 provides an excellent illustration of the choices that we have to make in life and the result of making wrong choices. The closing portion of the Lord's Sermon on the Mount included the illustration of two gates and two ways, two destinations, two groups of people, two types of trees, and two kinds of builders building on two types of foundations. This illustration was for the choice of holiness. Christ was drawing a clear delineation between the way that leads to destruction and the way of holiness which leads to life.

"No temptation has overtaken you except such as is common to man; but God is faithful, who will not allow you to be tempted beyond what you are able, but with the temptation will also make the way of escape, that you may be able to bear it."
(1 Corinthians 10:13)

To be sure, holiness does not bring an exemption from temptation. The choice of holiness comes with a cost, but you should not be surprised that the rise of temptation often arises through such things as poverty (see Proverbs 30:9; Matthew 4:2, 3), prosperity (see Proverbs 30:9; Matthew 4:8), and worldly glory (see Numbers 22:17; Daniel 4:30, 5:2; Matthew 4:8).

It should be noted that mistakes, infirmities, and involuntary offenses are inevitable as long as we are in the body. And while sin, by the keeping power of Christ, may be unavoidable throughout our regenerate lives, He also energizes our will to be able to stand

30

against every suggestion to act contrary to the will of God. There is no power on earth or in hell that can compel an individual to habitually sin who totally relies upon God to be kept from it. Through Christ, we are more than conquerors (see Romans 8:37). *"Where sin abounded, grace shall much more abound" (Romans 5:20)*. Holiness doesn't make anyone so secure that they cannot sin; however, it does provide all the elements of strength and stability.

What you should always remember is that God loves you with an everlasting love. You are His chosen vessel and you were crafted for His perfect work. Before sacrificing His life for you, He never compromised Himself or His anointing; even when He was faced with every temptation.

We can never compromise in our service to Him. We cannot forget that temptation is permitted to come–it was never, and will never be, restrained. You are mighty in the Kingdom of God. Stand in power and in God's loving care. His joy is your strength – this is your spiritual reality.

3. Implement Reverse Planning

We already know what God says about us, and in the end we win!

We should take what God says about us and apply it to our lives today. With our minds extended and knowing the end of the story, we have a mental image of the end and know how to plan to reach the destination that God has set for us.

When we visualize what God says about us and get a clear mental picture of the winner God made us to be, we can translate that to action steps that we can take right now. We can develop a step by step plan to reach the desired results. We can all extend our minds to the end and work backwards.

There is an expression that says, "hindsight is 20/20." This means that it is easy to know the right thing to do or say after something has already happened. But it is hard to predict the future on our own merit. Through the eyes of God we can see the impossible.

Hindsight represents thinking about things after they have happened and 20/20 represents perfect vision. Having 20/20 hindsight says that you can easily tell what you should have done in the past, but it's harder to decide what to do in the future. When you reflect on a situation, or look back (behind/"hind"), you can see more clearly what you should have said or done, than you could see when you were actually there and in the midst of it at the time.

Typically, a person using 20/20 hindsight is concerned with expressing the following:

- Don't worry about your past decisions; you can't change them now.
- Don't criticize the decision made; it was the best one that could have been made at the time.

When reflecting on our lives, we must be careful not to become legalistic in our thinking. We already know what God has said about us, and we have to take that information and begin to take action steps to apply His Word to our daily lives.

Not Legalism but Christ

"In Him you were also circumcised with the circumcision made without hands, by putting off the body of the sins of the flesh, by the circumcision of Christ, buried with Him in baptism, in which you also were raised with Him through faith in the working of God, who raised Him from the dead. And you, being dead in your trespasses and the uncircumcision of your flesh, He has made alive together with Him, having forgiven you all trespasses, having wiped out the handwriting of requirements that was against us, which was contrary to us. And He has taken it out of the way, having nailed it to the cross. Having disarmed principalities and powers, He made a public spectacle of them, triumphing over them in it." (Colossians 2:11-15)

Legalism[1] is the excessive and improper use of the Law (10 Commandments), and can take several forms. Some examples are:

- Where a person tries to keep the law in order to attain salvation–which can be a form of heresy (Romans 3:28, 4:5; Galatians 2:21).
- Where a person keeps the law in order to maintain their salvation–which can be through false doctrine.
- When a Christian judges other believers for not keeping certain codes of conduct that s/he thinks should be observed (Romans 14:1-12, 14:5).

We are taught not to judge others or debate issues. One person may desire to eat certain foods and another may not; or one may worship on a particular day of the week and another may not. Each person is allowed to be convinced in his/her own mind. As long as our freedom does not violate the Scriptures, then there should not be a problem.

Holiness and legalism are both heart issues. Holiness–like spiritual discipline–says, "I love God so much that I don't want to do anything that will displease Him. I <u>want</u> to change and become more like Christ." On the other hand, legalism says, "I <u>have</u> to do these things today otherwise God will not be pleased with me."

Like holiness, legalism has the same attitude of desire toward sin. The inner heart will still be in rebellion towards God, although the outer life looks like they are serving God. The difference is that someone who possesses true holiness will humbly accept rebuke and admonishment. They will desire to change and hate even the smallest sin in their lives. Conversely, the legalistic person may show anger towards those who try to give rebuke and admonishment because they feel there is nothing wrong in their lives.

Not Carnality but Christ

"If then you were raised with Christ, seek those things which are above, where Christ is, sitting at the right hand of God. Set your mind on things above, not on things on the earth. For you died, and your life is hidden with Christ in God. [4] When Christ who is our life appears, then you also will appear with Him in glory. Therefore put to death your members which are on the earth: fornication, uncleanness, passion, evil desire, and covetousness, which is idolatry. Because of these things the wrath of God is coming upon the sons of disobedience, in which you yourselves once walked when you lived in them. But now you yourselves are to put off all these: anger, wrath, malice, blasphemy, filthy language out of your mouth. Do not lie to one another, since you have put off the old man with his deeds, and have put on the new man who is renewed in knowledge according to the image of Him who created him, where there is neither Greek nor Jew,

*circumcised nor uncircumcised, barbarian, Scythian, slave nor
free, but Christ is all and in all." (Colossians 3:1-11)*

*"And I, brethren, could not speak to you as to spiritual people but
as to carnal, as to babes in Christ. I fed you with milk and not with
solid food; for until now you were not able to receive it, ad even
now you are still not able; for you are still carnal. For where there
are envy, strife, and divisions among you, are you not carnal and
behaving like mere men?" (1 Corinthians 3:1-3)*

Carnality[2], which is the opposite of holiness, carries several
symptoms:

- childishness and immaturity–the inability to absorb deep biblical
  truth
- envy–grudging others for their good fortune, success or quality
- strife–the result of envy causing division
- walking like men–spiritual pride and a walk like non-regenerate
  mankind

Galatians 5:16 provides the remedy for carnality. *"Walk in the
Spirit, and you shall not fulfill the lust of the flesh."* If we walk in
holiness and in the fellowship (the filling) of the Holy Spirit, we will
cease from being carnal. This involves the confession of sin.
Holiness requires that every time we recognize a sin in our lives, that
we confess it immediately. We then have the assurance of being
forgiven, and then the fellowship and filling of the Holy Spirit will
be restored to us.

*"If we confess our sins, He is faithful and just to forgive us our
sins and to cleanse us from all unrighteousness." (1 John 1:9)*

The Truth Shall Make You Free

*"Then Jesus said to those Jews who believed Him, "If you abide in
My word, you are My disciples indeed. And you shall know the
truth, and the truth shall make you free." They answered Him,
"We are Abraham's descendants, and have never been in bondage*

36

to anyone. How can You say, 'You will be made free'?" Jesus answered them, "Most assuredly, I say to you, whoever commits sin is a slave of sin. And a slave does not abide in the house forever, but a son abides forever. Therefore if the Son makes you free, you shall be free indeed." (John 8:31-36)

We have the unique opportunity to take what God says about us and apply it to our daily lives. With our minds extended and knowing the end of the story, we have a mental image of the end and we know how to plan to reach the destination that God has set for us.

The person who lives in holiness knows of God's divine truth and freely walks in obedience to the Word. Moreover, this person has no fear of the bondage and slavery of sin. Slavery in this case refers to habitual sin–when one sins and appears to not have any control or ability to abstain from it.

The life of holiness is not a walk according to the flesh nor of condemnation, but that of the Holy Spirit. There is no sin that a true follower of Christ can commit–whether past, present, or future–that can be held against him/her, because the penalty for that sin was already paid for by Christ Himself; and righteous (holiness) was then transmitted (imputed) to that follower. There is no sin that can ever reverse this divine decision (see Romans 8:1-2). You are, indeed, made free by Christ Jesus.

The Spirit, Not the Letter

"And we have such trust through Christ toward God. Not that we are sufficient of ourselves to think of anything as being from ourselves, but our sufficiency is from God, who also made us sufficient as ministers of the new covenant, not of the letter but of the Spirit; for the letter kills, but the Spirit gives life." (2 Corinthians 3:4-6)

Glory of the New Covenant

"But if the ministry of death, written and engraved on stones, was glorious, so that the children of Israel could not look steadily at the face of Moses because of the glory of his countenance, which glory was passing away, how will the ministry of the Spirit not be more glorious? For if the ministry of condemnation had glory, the ministry of righteousness exceeds much more in glory. For even what was made glorious had no glory in this respect, because of the glory that excels. For if what is passing away was glorious, what remains is much more glorious. Therefore, since we have such hope, we use great boldness of speech— unlike Moses, who put a veil over his face so that the children of Israel could not look steadily at the end of what was passing away. But their minds were blinded. For until this day the same veil remains unlifted in the reading of the Old Testament, because the veil is taken away in Christ. But even to this day, when Moses is read, a veil lies on their heart. Nevertheless when one turns to the Lord, the veil is taken away. Now the Lord is the Spirit; and where the Spirit of the Lord is, there is liberty. But we all, with unveiled face, beholding as in a mirror the glory of the Lord, are being transformed into the same image from glory to glory, just as by the Spirit of the Lord."
(2 Corinthians 3:4-18)

It is the Spirit and the Word of God that gives life; but the letter of legalism and hypocrisy is what kills (in the spiritual sense). This legalism is to the superficial act of abiding by the rules and customs of the law that then misses the most basic requirement of holiness and distorting its original intention; which was to make a person aware of his/her sinfulness.

We should not be misled, however, because the law of God is not a bad thing. It does reveal God's divine standard. As we compare ourselves to that standard, we should be able to accurately identify sin, which is the failure to meet the standard (or missing the mark).

"Therefore He who supplies the Spirit to you and works miracles among you, does He do it by the works of the law, or by the hearing of faith?–just as Abraham 'believed God, and it was accounted to

him for righteousness.' Therefore know that only those who are of faith are sons of Abraham. And the Scripture, foreseeing that God would justify the Gentiles by faith, preached the gospel to Abraham beforehand, saying, 'In you all the nations shall be blessed.' So then those who are of faith are blessed with believing Abraham."
(Galatians 3:5-9)

Abraham knew exactly what the destiny would be for his family and for his ancestors. Those who are of the seed of Abraham have the assurance of receiving the blessings of justification by faith. As a direct result, those same blessings are now poured out on all because of Christ Jesus.

Abraham's faith represented the perfect example of true belief in God. In spite of what others may have thought of him or how foolish he may have seemed to them, his true love for God superseded his natural affection for his family or friends. He had no problem leaving the place of comfort to allow himself to be led to the place of promise and destiny. He knew what he was purposed to do, and he was determined to fulfill it.

"So the LORD said, 'I will destroy man whom I have created from the face of the earth, both man and beast, creeping thing and birds of the air, for I am sorry that I have made them.' But Noah found grace in the eyes of the LORD. ....And Noah did according to all that the LORD commanded him." (Genesis 6:7-8; 7:5)

God knew that no one would believe in what Noah was doing nor the reasons why, therefore, He made it clear that Noah was not acting on just his acts of good works alone. Noah was not legalistically obedient to God. God found favor in Noah because of his holiness. Noah was favored by God because he was obedient to the Lord, and was humble and sought after God. He was aware of his own inherent sin nature and the fact that there was no way possible to be in a position to forgive his own sins. Therefore, he humbly turned to God for mercy and grace in hopes of a restored personal relationship. Noah sought after holiness before God.

".... Then men began to call on the name of the LORD." (Genesis 4:26[b])

"Then I heard a loud voice saying in heaven, "Now salvation, and strength, and the kingdom of our God, and the power of His Christ have come, for the accuser of our brethren, who accused them before our God day and night, has been cast down.' And they overcame him by the blood of the Lamb and by the word of their testimony, and they did not love their lives to the death." (Revelation 12:10-11)

4. Develop and Deploy Kingdom Action Steps

We are now at the place where we have identified where we are supposed to be, and the challenge is to now ascertain the origin of any gaps or openings. A conscious effort to develop an action plan must be made, as well as a method of deployment. Our holiness thinking should be extended to a place where we become ready to act on the plan of holiness.

"Pursue peace with all people, and holiness, without which no one will see the LORD." (Hebrews 12:14)

"but as He who called you is holy, you also be holy in all your conduct, because it is written, 'Be holy, for I am holy.'" (1 Peter 1:15-16)

For some people, holiness may seem to be an impossibility—something that is too high to attain. Yet we are called to be holy because the God we serve is a holy God, and we were created in His image and likeness.

Holiness is not so much about how you appear to others, but rather where you are actually headed. There is a definite path of holiness (a narrow path), and it is up to each of us to be able to walk that path.

This is a walk that we must be consciously willing to take, on a daily basis.

In order to be certain that you are progressing in the right direction on the way to holiness, and not just marching in place, there are some life 'guideposts' or road markers for which you should be on the lookout. As you progress on the path of holiness, you should desire to do the following[1]:

- Progressing to a place where you become more fully centered on the will of God.
    o You begin to yearn to be in service to the Lord in all things, and at all times, because it is in Him that you "live and move and have your being" (Acts 17:28).
- Becoming increasingly aware of the things in your life that keep you from Him.
- Developing a hunger and a desire to serve Him (1 Peter 2:5).
    o Your prayer life begins to increase, you desire to help the poor and needy, and you are now more readily acceptable to carrying the cross of Christ.

Character of the New Man

"Therefore, as the elect of God, holy and beloved, put on tender mercies, kindness, humility, meekness, longsuffering; bearing with one another, and forgiving one another, if anyone has a complaint against another; even as Christ forgave you, so you also must do.
But above all these things put on love, which is the bond of perfection. And let the peace of God rule in your hearts, to which also you were called in one body; and be thankful. Let the word of Christ dwell in you richly in all wisdom, teaching and admonishing one another in psalms and hymns and spiritual songs, singing with grace in your hearts to the Lord. And whatever you do in word or deed, do all in the name of the Lord Jesus, giving thanks to God the Father through Him." (Colossians 3:12-17)

It is possible to live in total holiness, but there are some things to be aware of. It's important to remember that you cannot modify holiness to be something that you can 'do.' Holiness is something that God causes you to become. You simply receive it or reject it. There is a process, and it is likely that during that process of walking into holiness, you will slip, you will fall, you will confess your sins, and God will forgive you of those sins.

There are some who have lost the hope of holiness, and a direct result, they have redefined holiness. The Word clearly tells us that anything that is not of faith is sin. That means that sin can be anything that we think, say, or do that God has not led us to do and that He has not done through us.

It's usually at this point that we miss most of His leading and then insert our own fleshly selves into the process of walking into holiness. There is only one way for you to 'do' righteousness–that is by allowing Jesus to do righteousness within you. This is actually what grace does–it does its perfect work in you.

The Holy Spirit assists us in walking in holiness by giving us the ability to walk in righteousness. The first step in this process is putting on the new man. Putting on the new man requires putting on tender mercies (the right heart). In the physical sense, the heart denotes the physical intestines; however, when used figuratively, it denotes deep emotions such as tenderness and affection.

What is significant about putting on the heart of the new man is that before that can even happen, we have to first be baptized as the Word commands. Colossians 2:11-13 lets us know that we are circumcised with the circumcision of Christ, buried with Him in baptism, and resurrected through faith by the working of God. We are made alive together with Jesus and are forgiven of our transgressions.

Next, we can put on the new man and the heart of the new man because we have been made new in Christ Jesus (Colossians 3:10, 12). Because we are now new creatures in Christ, we are able to put aside sin and put on the new man. The Apostle Paul lets us know in Ephesians 4:22-24 that we are to *"lay aside the old self, which is being corrupted in accordance with the lusts of deceit ... and put on the new self, which in the likeness of God has been created in righteousness and holiness of the truth."*

43

The characteristics of the new man include[2]:

- The ability to *bear* with one another and *forgive* as Christ has forgiven us.
- The ability to *put on love*, which is the perfect bond of *unity* and unifies us with the brethren.
- The ability to allow the *peace* of Christ rule in our hearts and be *thankful*.
- The ability to allow the *Word of Christ to richly dwell within us.*
- Doing it *all in the Name of the Lord Jesus*, giving *thanks* through Him to the Father.
- The ability to *subject ourselves to human authority*, and *exercise authority over others according to the will of God*–both at home and on our jobs. And *whatever we do, we do heartily as for the Lord.*
- The ability to dedicate and *devote ourselves to prayer*, keeping alert and with an attitude of thanksgiving.
- The ability to *conduct ourselves with wisdom toward others*, and make the most of the opportunity to witness to them.
- The ability to allow our *speech to be with grace*, as though it were seasoned with salt, so that we will know how to respond.

To appear to be holy, some may emulate holiness in order to impress others, or even ourselves, by trying to obey a set of rules, laws, or principles. However, this usually leads to a false hope, to hypocrisy and to spiritual deadness.

We cannot deny the reality that our humanness can cause us problems in the walk of holiness.

- Thoughts enter our minds that are not always pure.
- We get angry.
- We become discouraged.
- There are times when we are not flowing in the anointing of God.
- There are times when God is not the most prominent focus of our minds.

However, the process that brings us to the point of walking in total holiness is in knowing that God's Spirit is given to us and we learn to yield our minds to Him.

As we yield:

- Our minds are renewed by the Spirit (He does the work).
- He thinks His thoughts through us (He is the source of all wisdom, knowledge and understanding).
- He speaks His Word through us (we start to speak as oracles of God).
- He does His work through us (we never do our own will–only His will).

There will be times when we will see a moment of His glory in our lives. That's because the process of holiness is a continuous one. We are mostly in a process of coming into His glory, and His forgiveness is a continual and perpetual covering of our missteps.

God's desire is to continue to flow through us until we are conformed into His image in every facet of our being. When that happens, we will be transfigured by the renewing of our minds.

Light Bearers

"Therefore, my beloved, as you have always obeyed, not as in my presence only, but now much more in my absence, work out your own salvation with fear and trembling; for it is God who works in you both to will and to do for His good pleasure. Do all things without complaining and disputing, that you may become blameless and harmless, children of God without fault in the midst of a crooked and perverse generation, among whom you shine as lights in the world, holding fast the word of life, so that I may rejoice in the day of Christ that I have not run in vain or labored in vain." (Philippians 2:12-16)

The path of holiness is one of increasing light; just as a sunrise begins with the faint glow of dawn and proceeds to the majesty of the noonday. By bringing in the light of Christ through holiness, we

45

become light bearers. As light bearers, we are empowered by the Holy Spirit and are the anchors for the light of Christ with every step we take. We have the ability to shine as lights and to show our character, which exemplifies Christ, to a lost, dark, and dying world.

Light has the ability to illuminate and make everything visible. As light bearers, we have the unique opportunity to be able to extend the light of the Word of God and of salvation to the unsaved so that they too may be transformed from the children of darkness into the children of God's holy and marvelous light. Those who consistently walk in holiness gain ever-increasing light; just as a sunrise begins with a faint glow over the horizon and then proceeds to the splendor of a noonday.

"The path of the just is like the shining sun, that shines ever brighter unto the perfect day." (Proverbs 4:18)

"I thank my God upon every remembrance of you, always in every prayer of mine making request for you all with joy, for your fellowship in the gospel from the first day until now, being confident of this very thing, that He who has begun a good work in you will complete it until the day of Jesus Christ." (Philippians 1:3-6)

God began His great and perfect work of salvation in you before He formed you in your mother's womb; and He intends to finish that perfect work. In ancient times, dishonest pottery dealers would fill the cracks in their inferior pots with wax before glazing and painting them, making it difficult to detect any defects in their workmanship. The only way to prevent being defrauded was to hold the pot up to the sunlight, making the cracks visible.

The walk of holiness requires that you be sincere and without offense; that you should be able to be tested by the light, and that your integrity would be intact, and not lead others to sin.

Unity through Humility

There are a lot of people–even Christian believers–who only live to make a good impression on others or to please themselves. Those who walk in holiness are encouraged to love one another and to be on one accord with spiritual humility. When we work together, caring for the problems of others as if they were our own problems, then we demonstrate Christ's example of putting others before ourselves, and we experience unity.

"Therefore if there is any consolation in Christ, if any comfort of love, if any fellowship of the Spirit, if any affection and mercy, fulfill my joy by being like-minded, having the same love, being of one accord, of one mind. Let nothing be done through selfish ambition or conceit, but in lowliness of mind let each esteem others better than himself. Let each of you look out not only for his own interests, but also for the interests of others." (Philippians 2:1-4)

Unity through humility in the walk of holiness means that we are to lay aside selfishness and to treat others with respect and courtesy. By considering others' interests as more important than our own, we are linked to Christ–the true example of humility. Failing to guard against selfishness, prejudice or jealousy leads to conflict and disagreements. However, the ability to show genuine interest in others is a positive step forward in maintaining unity among other believers.

Christ was our perfect example. He was humble and willing to give up His rights and serve others, in obedience to the Father. The walk of holiness demonstrates having a servant's attitude and being able to serve others out of love for God and for others–not out of guilt or fear.

The key to remember is that you can choose your attitude. You can approach life either by being served or you can look for opportunities to serve others.

The Humbled and Exalted Christ

"Let this mind be in you which was also in Christ Jesus, who, being in the form of God, did not consider it robbery to be equal with God, but made Himself of no reputation, taking the form of a bondservant, and coming in the likeness of men. And being found in appearance as a man, He humbled Himself and became obedient to the point of death, even the death of the cross. Therefore God also has highly exalted Him and given Him the name which is above every name, that at the name of Jesus every knee should bow, of those in heaven, and of those on earth, and of those under the earth, and that every tongue should confess that Jesus Christ is Lord, to the glory of God the Father." (Philippians 2:5-11)

Humility says that we do not live to make a good impression on others. It says that we are thinking of others as being better than ourselves. We have to show an interest in others and in what they are doing, and not just our own affairs.

The attitude we choose to exhibit should be the same as that of Christ. Although He was God, He did not demand and cling to His rights as God. In fact, He took the humble position of a slave when He appeared in human form. While in human form, He further humbled Himself by dying on the cross. It was for this reason that the Father raised Him up to the heights of heaven, gave Him a Name that is above all names; so that at the Name of Jesus, every knee will bow and every tongue will confess that He is Lord–to the glory of God the Father.

"Rejoice in the Lord always. Again I will say, rejoice! Let your gentleness be known to all men. The Lord is at hand. Be anxious for nothing, but in everything by prayer and supplication, with thanksgiving, let your requests be made known to God; and the peace of God, which surpasses all understanding, will guard your hearts and minds through Christ Jesus." (Philippians 4:4-8)

Meditate on These Things

"Finally, brethren, whatever things are true, whatever things are noble, whatever things are just, whatever things are pure, whatever things are lovely, whatever things are of good report, if there is any virtue and if there is anything praiseworthy—meditate on these things. The things which you learned and received and heard and saw in me, these do, and the God of peace will be with you."
(Philippians 4:8-9)

Every believer is expected to walk in holiness and in the power of God. However, most appear to be unable to see themselves in a place where they operate in the fullness of holiness and the power of God.

We should never measure our spirituality by the amount of miracles, signs, and wonders that occur in our lives. Miracles are designed to change the life of the person that needs the miracle. The same thing applies to healings. Healing and miracles are not to proof that we are men and women of God. We are men and women of God because God says that we are. Consequently, we can be holy because the holy God has declared us to be holy as He is holy.[1]

The question that should be asked and answered is simply, what is the secret to walking in holiness and in the power of God? Simply stated, there has to be obedience from your heart to the known will of God in order for holiness and for His power to manifest.

Think of it from God's point of view. Why would God endorse a program that was not His own? Why would God anoint a vessel for His divine service that thinks it can go in any direction it chooses and then expects His power to show up?

Consider how a remote control device works. When you think about a remote control, you think of controlling something from a distance and not having to jump up and down to make any adjustments or change channels. Also, if you want to see your favorite program, you can simply program your device to record—even if you are not at home.

Most people want a controlled environment. We want what we want to happen, when we want it, and how we want it. But living in this type of controlled environment does not allow the Holy Spirit to take you to where God wants to lead you. We want to control our own lives, but we fail to realize that there is only so much we can do. Releasing our lives into His hands causes us to totally rely upon God. The walk of holiness becomes a matter of complete trust.

Learning how to trust is a major factor for many of us. God wants us to fully trust in Him. That requires that we take our hands off the remote. We have to stop pushing the buttons. We have to allow God to make our choices for us—knowing that He knows what is best and that He is able to protect us from all evil.

This also means that we have to keep our lives clean. We have to be obedient—even if others around us are not being obedient. Avoid sin—and if we do fall into sin, then we only need to acknowledge that we have sinned against Him, confess it, and ask for forgiveness.

5. Adapt to a Kingdom Character

Kingdom Agenda

"Then God said, 'Let Us make man in Our image, according to Our likeness; let them have dominion over the fish of the sea, over the birds of the air, and over the cattle, over all the earth and over every creeping thing that creeps on the earth.' So God created man in His own image; in the image of God He created him; male and female He created them. Then God blessed them, and God said to them, 'Be fruitful and multiply; fill the earth and subdue it; have dominion over the fish of the sea, over the birds of the air, and over every living thing that moves on the earth." (Genesis 1:26-28)

God had us on His mind before the foundation of the earth. He had an agenda, a set idea of how things would work and flow, and we were part of His agenda. God had a kingdom of rulers in mind and that rule included us. God is the Supreme Ruler and Creator. He made everything for His glory.

God made us in His image (spiritual nature) and likeness (functionality) to rule over this earth. He put man (and woman) in charge of everything He made and gave us the ability to have dominion. His agenda was for us to be His kings and priests (1 Peter 2:9 and Revelation 1:5-6) under Him as the ultimate ruler of all things through Christ Jesus. He set us up as His agents, or ambassadors, over all the earth and everything on it. He made us in His image so that we could do the same things that Jesus did as our example on earth (John 14:12)–but greater; much greater.

It is interesting to me that we are called to have a kingly agenda, yet we are not fully aware of how to do it. That is why we have the Holy Spirit to guide us and show us the way. The Holy Spirit will serve as our Teacher, our Revealer, our Counselor; and He will give us wisdom, understanding, and might to do the task. Actually, it is not by our power or by our might, but all things can, and should, be done by the Holy Spirit (Zechariah 4:6), says the Lord over all the armies of heaven and earth.

"So He said to them, 'When you pray, say: Our Father in heaven, hallowed be Your name. Your kingdom come. Your will be done on earth as it is in heaven." (Luke 11:2-3)

Since it is God's Kingdom agenda, the Word lets us know that we can pray for His agenda to be implemented and planted firmly in this earth. When Jesus was speaking with His disciples, He taught them how to pray for God's agenda to permeate the earth. He taught them to pray for the Kingdom to come on earth. That lets us know that God's Kingdom agenda for earth is for us to look just like heaven. We play a vital role as partakers and partners with Christ in making this happen. Christ taught us to bind everything that is not like heaven and make earth look like heaven through the words we speak (Matthew 18:18). He also states that we should do it together in agreement with others, and He promised to be there with us making it happen (Matthew 18:19-20).

"He answered and said to them, 'Because it has been given to you to know the mysteries of the kingdom of heaven, but to them it is has not been given. For whoever has, to him more will be given, and he will have abundance; but whoever does not have even what he has will be taken away from him.'" (Matthew 13:11-12)

The Kingdom is a mystery, meaning that there is a requirement that it be revealed and made known. The mystery was not given in ages past, but will be given to faithful believers.

I worked over twenty years at NASA–Marshall Space Flight Center (MSFC) in Huntsville, Alabama. At MSFC, we worked on propulsion element for the U. S. space shuttle. I also worked in experiments that flew in the manifest bay of the space shuttle. Many experiments that helped with medical research, technology, and science were deployed in the manifest bay. Many breakthroughs occurred as a result of space research. Many mysteries about were resolved in space, including how the effects of space atmosphere will assist in the graceful aging process, and how the effects of space on bones and muscles assists in medical research.

The Kingdom of Heaven holds many mysteries for our benefit on earth and for our eternity. Unlike NASA where mysteries were revealed through the efforts of humankind, God reveals them to us through the Holy Spirit, and He unfolds His magnificent glory to us. God is a spirit and the mysteries of His kingdom are revealed in the spiritual realm–far above the realm where a space shuttle can fly.

"Jesus answered and said to him, 'Most assuredly, I say to you, unless one is born again, he cannot see the kingdom of God.'"
(Matthew 3:3)

In order for us to see the Kingdom, we must first be born again. Seeing the Kingdom of God is part of God's agenda for us on earth. We come to the new birth through Jesus Christ, our Lord. We must confess with our mouth and believe in our heart to be saved. After that, we should be baptized with water as an outward sign of our inward confession.

"And Jesus came and spoke to them, saying, 'All authority has been given to Me in heaven and on earth. Go therefore and make disciples of all the nations, baptizing them in the name of the Father and of the Son and of the Holy Spirit, teaching them to

observe all thins that I have commanded you; and lo, I am with you always, even to the end of the age.'" (Matthew 28:18-20)

"And He said to them, 'Go into all the world and preach the gospel to every creature. He who believes and is baptized will be saved; but he who does not believe will be condemned. And these signs will follow those who believe: In My name they will cast out demons; they will speak with new tongues; they will take up serpents; and if they drink anything deadly, it will by no means hurt them; they will lay hands on the sick, and they will recover.'"
(Mark 16:15-18)

I recently spent a week in Houston, Texas and attended an Advancing Minorities Interest in Engineering (AMIE) meeting. One of AMIE's goals is to get K-12 minority students interested in the Science, Technology, Engineering, and Math (STEM) fields and careers. Part of that meeting included a visit to Prairieview A&M University to talk to students majoring in Engineering and Computer Science. While on a tour of the Engineering facility, I had an opportunity to learn many things. One of the most interesting parts of the tour was the "Store Front" where students actually had jobs to support NASA's missions and objectives. Their assistance was in helping NASA scientists and engineers solve problems associated environmental issues, electromechanical systems, as well as other engineering and computer systems. Another interesting area was where students worked with simulated moon dirt and simulated mars dirt that could be used in developing structures for space applications and space living. WOW!! How awesome is that–our kids are really doing it!!

Anyway, while I was there, I asked why God made scientists, engineers, computers, buildings, nurses, doctors, and the like. I really wanted to know why He made me an engineer, manager, and a preacher all in one. After a short dialogue with a believer colleague from Purdue, God revealed this profound answer: He made us this way and gave us the experiences in life for the following:

1. To know that Jesus is Lord, and that every knee and everything with a name shall bow to Him.

54

2. Because it was in His plan for us to have the best path to find Him and to be sure He is the One doing it for us and through us.
3. To know Him in diverse ways.
4. To remember that He, and He alone, is God.
5. To build His Kingdom and tear down Satan's counterfeit kingdom.
6. Make Him known throughout the world as the great commission mandates.

Inspire Others

"And again He began to teach by the sea. And a great multitude was gathered to Him, so that He got into a boat and sat in it on the sea; and the whole multitude was on the land facing the sea."
(Mark 4:1)

Before getting to the "how," in terms of inspiring others, let's start with the "why." The answer actually lies in the construction of the words "inspire" and "Spirit." Both of these words are rooted in the Latin word "spirare" which means "to breathe." So, when looking at the word inspire, you can see that it is broken down into the phrase to "breathe into." Inspiring others means, therefore, that you should be breathing life into them.

This is the greatest gift that can be offered to someone. When you are inspiring others, you are literally giving them life. Inspiration has the ability to multiply, and it has the same outward rippling affect as a pebble thrown into a quiet body of water. When you allow God to be your inspiration, then you have the ability to touch a multitude of lives. Choosing the path of inspiration can be rewarding and fulfilling.

Jesus was the greatest source of inspiration of all time. Scriptures reflect this in many ways. Jesus was 100% God and 100% man as He walked on this earth. He was certainly inspirational with His way to affect the masses and even the twelve. He was a great Healer, Deliverer, Comforter, and the list goes on.

55

Jesus came to show us how to do it. Kingdom character includes inspiration. You may be a person who loves to inspire youth into action through innovative biblical teaching, or you may be a person who spends time one-on-one with the elderly inspiring them to hold on to God's unchanging hand.

Godly inspiration is needed today more than ever. With so many distractions in this world like work, shopping, video games, dating, Facebook, twitter, distractions and other things, someone needs to stand tall and just inspire.

So one might ask, just how do you inspire others? It is simple. Pick your favorite scripture about how Jesus did His miracles, your favorite Psalm about the awesomeness of God, your favorite story about how God helped you, share it with others, and you will inspire them. The Word of God carries the anointing of God, and the Holy Spirit will do the drawing. The scripture promises that if you lift up the Name of Jesus, He will do the drawing unto Himself (John 12:32). Being drawn by Jesus is inspirational.

"But when they believed Philip as he preached the things concerning the kingdom of God and the name of Jesus Christ, both men and women were baptized. Then Simon himself also believed; and when he was baptized he continued with Philip, and was amazed, seeing the miracles and signs which were done." (Acts 8:12-13)

Philip had an amazing way of preaching and teaching things concerning the Kingdom of God through the name of Jesus. Men and women from all around came to hear about Jesus and were baptized. When you teach about the Kingdom of God and the Name of Jesus Christ, others will be inspired. In addition, people will be amazed with your teaching and will also be amazed to see that miracles, signs and wonders may be done around you.

56

"And he went into the synagogue and spoke boldly for three months, reasoning and persuading concerning the things of the kingdom of God." (Acts 19:8)

"So when they had appointed him a day, many came to him at his lodging, to whom he explained and solemnly testified of the kingdom of God, persuading them concerning Jesus from both the Law of Moses and the Prophets, from morning till evening." (Acts 28:23)

Paul was not always well received by the leaders and others in the synagogue when he preached Jesus as Christ and the resurrection of Christ. But Paul was not discouraged. We should not be discouraged when others are not inspired by our words. Keep moving forward and God will put you in the path of people who will be inspired.

Paul also preached and taught the Kingdom of God both in prison and his home. Many were saved as a result of the inspiration of the Holy Spirit through Paul's preaching and teaching. You will do the same in your community, church, and at home.

Do not stop…your audience is just a step or two away!

Never Give Up

"Then Nebuchadnezzar, in rage and fury, gave the command to bring Shadrach, Meshach, and Abed-Nego. So they brought these men before the king. Nebuchadnezzar spoke, saying to them, 'Is it true, Shadrach, Meshach, and Abed-Nego, that you do not serve my gods or worship the gold image which I have set up? Now if you are ready at the time you hear the sound of the horn, flute, harp, lyre, and psaltery, in symphony with all kinds of music, and you fall down and worship the image which I have made, good! But if you do not worship, you shall be cast immediately into the midst of a burning fiery furnace. And who is the god who will deliver you from my hands?' Shadrach, Meshach, and Abed-Nego answered and said to the king, 'O Nebuchadnezzar, we have no need to answer you in this matter. If that is the case, our God

57

whom we serve is able to deliver us from the burning fiery furnace,
and He will deliver us from your hand, O king. But if not, let it be
known to you, O king, that we do not serve your gods, nor will we
worship the gold image which you have set up.' Then
Nebuchadnezzar was full of fury, and the expression on his face
changed toward Shadrach, Meshach, and Abed-Nego. He spoke
and commanded that they heat the furnace seven times more than
it was usually heated. And he commanded certain mighty men of
valor who were in his army to bind Shadrach, Meshach, and Abed-
Nego, and cast them into the burning fiery furnace. Then these
men were bound in their coats, their trousers, their turbans, and
their other garments, and were cast into the midst of the burning
fiery furnace. Therefore, because the king's command was urgent,
and the furnace exceedingly hot, the flame of the fire killed those
men who took up Shadrach, Meshach, and Abed-Nego. And these
three men, Shadrach, Meshach, and Abed-Nego, fell down bound
into the midst of the burning fiery furnace. Then King
Nebuchadnezzar was astonished; and he rose in haste and spoke,
saying to his counselors, 'Did we not cast three men bound into the
midst of the fire?' They answered and said to the king, 'True, O
king.' 'Look!' he answered, 'I see four men loose, walking in the
midst of the fire; and they are not hurt, and the form of the fourth
is like the Son of God.'" (Daniel 3:13-25)

Whew–that fire must have been really hot!! I was just outside standing by the grill. In fact, my cloths smell like smoke from burgers and hot dogs being cooked on the grill. Okay, okay–we had chicken too (healthy food)!! No talking about the Daniel fast right now (smile)...

These three Hebrew boys got placed into the fiery furnace with their clothes, turbans and other garments, and were cast into the fire. When they were retrieved, they didn't even smell like smoke. Here I am smelling like burgers, and the men of God in this passage didn't smell at all. What a mighty God we serve!!

This story has spiritual and physical implications. Kingdom character gives us the ability to "never give up"–even during adverse situations. Spiritually, the enemy will seek to put you in a situation where the heat is turned up in your life. This situation usually manifests in the physical world as a problem that intimidates you. The problem will usually seem tougher than what you are able to handle; but with God, you can make it.

I really like the attitude of the three Hebrew boys:

"Shadrach, Meshach, and Abed-Nego answered and said to the king, 'O Nebuchadnezzar, we have no need to answer you in this matter. If that is the case, our God whom we serve is able to deliver us from the burning fiery furnace, and He will deliver us from your hand, O king. But if not, let it be known to you, O king, that we do not serve your gods, nor will we worship the gold image which you have set up.'" (Daniel 3:16-18)

No matter what the problem (heat), God is well able to deliver you from your circumstance. When you give up, you have taken the stance that you are defeated. That is a disillusion sent to trick you. There is nothing too hard for God; absolutely nothing.

So, you need a job, peace of mind, your husband to understand you better, your child to act godly, you need rent money, a car, and a place to live. God is able. If your boss is giving you a hard time about your work, your company is undergoing layoffs, and the economy is going under, God is able. Never give up. Giving up means that you quit, you're finished, you're putting up with your circumstances, and you are down to nothing. Never means never! If you are at a place like Shadrach, Meshach, and Abed-Nego, do like they did. Take a stand for God. If you do not take a stand for God, then you have given up. When you stand for God, He can, and will, deliver you.

Also, remember there is no gray area, you cannot ride the fence nor remain neutral. Not standing for and with God essentially means you are agreeing to nullify your authority and position of power. This destroys your effectiveness in the Kingdom and offers the enemy an opportunity to wreak havoc in your life (read Exodus 32:22-33).

Give Cheerfully

"Give, and it will be given to you: good measure, pressed down, shaken together, and running over will be put into your bosom. For with the same measure that you use, it will be measured back to you." (Luke 6:38)

"But this I say: He who sows sparingly will also reap sparingly, and he who sows bountifully will also reap bountifully. So let each one give as he purposes in his heart, not grudgingly or of necessity; for God loves a cheerful giver. And God is able to make all grace abound toward you, that you, always having all sufficiency in all things, may have an abundance for every good work." (2 Corinthians 9:6-8)

The question that should be asked about giving is, when we give, to whom are we giving? When we give, we are to give according to God's Word to Him; not to the church and not to a specific person. In His Word, when God asks us to give, He is asking for us to give to Him and Him alone. When we give to God, it is God who gives back to us in return. He uses us as vessels and instruments to give to others on His behalf.

One week day, I went to a local burger restaurant to get my son one of his favorite meals—chicken strips. It had been a long day and I wanted to make sure he had something to eat. When we pulled into the parking lot, I noticed a blonde-haired gentleman sitting on the curb with his face buried into his hands. He was shaking his head from side to side, and also I noticed him lifting his hands up toward heaven as if to make a continued petition. God spoke to my heart and told me to let the man know that I would buy him something to eat and that I would be going through the drive-thru and would bring it back around to him in a few minutes. I decided that I would surprise him, and ignored my instructions from God.

As I went around to the drive-through, I asked for the meal for my son and also asked for three sandwiches (I figured that the man would be hungry later and decided to purchase more than one sandwich). As I pulled around to the front of the restaurant where the man had been sitting, I noticed he was not on the curb. It was dark, but I looked around to find the man with the blonde hair. I didn't see him at all. Immediately I prayed to God, asked for forgiveness and asked that God would show me where the man was. After my prayer, I looked around another parking lot, and there he was walking in the faint darkness. I drove up to him with an apology for not obeying my original instructions and let him know I had purchased dinner for him. I gave him the bag with three sandwiches in it. He said, "You bought three? I have two other friends who are hungry too...thank you!" He lifted his hands up to heaven and said, "Thank you, Lord," and then he grabbed me and said, "Don't stop believing in Jesus, lady. Don't stop!" He further said that he had asked for food from God and wondered why his prayer wasn't answered.

My giving gave a meal to three people that day. Since that time, I have been given more and more opportunities to feed and seed into God's Kingdom. He keeps giving back more to me every time I give. I am so in awe of God!!

Isaac obediently gave to God by planting into good soil and reaped a hundred fold harvest (Genesis 26:12). The widow gave her last to God (Mark 12:41-44). Jesus was pleased with her giving and commented to the local leaders. Is your giving at the level where Jesus, sitting at the right hand of God, is commenting on it? Are you like Cornelius and has your alms (giving) being brought up before the Lord and a memorial (Acts 10:4)?

Dominate Territory and Destiny

"Then God said, 'Let Us make man in Our image, according to Our likeness; let them have dominion over the fish of the sea, over the birds of the air, and over the cattle, over all the earth and over every creeping thing that creeps on the earth. '" (Genesis 1:26)

"Every place that the sole of your foot will tread upon I have given you, as I said to Moses. From the wilderness and this Lebanon as far as the great river, the River Euphrates, all the land of the Hittites, and to the Great Sea toward the going down of the sun,

61

shall be your territory. No man shall be able to stand before you all the days of your life; as I was with Moses, so I will be with you. I will not leave you nor forsake you. Be strong and of good courage, for to this people you shall divide as an inheritance the land which I swore to their fathers to give them. Only be strong and very courageous, that you may observe to do according to all the law which Moses My servant commanded you; do not turn from it to the right hand or to the left, that you may prosper wherever you go. This Book of the Law shall not depart from your mouth, but you shall meditate in it day and night, that you may observe to do according to all that is written in it. For then you will make your way prosperous, and then you will have good success. Have I not commanded you? Be strong and of good courage; do not be afraid, nor be dismayed, for the LORD your God is with you wherever you go." (Joshua 1:3-9)

I am from the South. In 2003, God asked me to leave my 20+ years place of employment, family and friends to move to the great southwest; the big city of Tucson. To make the transition better for my family, He provided an excellent job to my husband and me in the city. Also as a minister, God sent me to a wonderful church to learn and grow. Before I moved to Tucson, God told me that I would be asked to do something by Him that would be the most beautiful thing that I could do for Him. I thought to myself that the assignment that God would give me would involve traveling around the globe preaching and teaching His divine Word.

Well, that wasn't quite how it happened. In the fall of 2007, the call came all right. That call was for me to go a few miles away (not across country) to a small local church to serve. God told me my destiny would be determined by being at that church.

When my family went, we really enjoyed serving in the church. I never thought in my lifetime that I would become pastor. Within a few months, the presiding pastor suddenly became ill and could no longer serve the church. Long story short, I was asked to be the pastor of the church, and the rest is history.

The territory that I was to dominate was located just a few miles away. I was to dominate by establishing renewed vision for the church, updating and enhancing the church building, and introduce a more diverse style of worship. My territory was to engage in teaching new members about the Kingdom of God and how they are purposed to do the same within our community. The church had faithful members when I became pastor and now that church is growing and more spiritual each day!

"And from the days of John the Baptist until now the kingdom of heaven suffers violence, and the violent take it by force."
(Matthew 11:12))

"But if I cast out demons by the Spirit of God, surely the kingdom of God has come upon you. Or how can one enter a strong man's house and plunder his goods, unless he first binds the strong man? And then he will plunder his house. He who is not with Me is against Me, and he who does not gather with Me scatters abroad."
(Matthew 12:28-30)

"Behold, I give you the authority to trample on serpents and scorpions, and over all the power of the enemy, and nothing shall by any means hurt you. Nevertheless do not rejoice in this, that the spirits are subject to you, but rather rejoice because your names are written in heaven." (Luke 10:19-20)

While at my current church, God is training me to know true authority as an ambassador for Christ. He is teaching me a greater vision that He has for the church through the healing and deliverance ministry. I believe that every believer should be free to serve God in an awesome way without any hindrances or outside influences from evil. I further believe we can execute the Word of God against evil in our lives and in the territory we are assigned.

We all have the authority to take territory back for the Kingdom through the Name of Jesus and the power of the Holy Spirit.

Open to Learn

"But seek first the kingdom of God and His righteousness, and all these things shall be added to you." (Matthew 6:33)

"At that time Jesus answered and said, 'I thank You, Father, Lord of heaven and earth, that You have hidden these things from the wise and prudent and have revealed them to babes. Even so, Father, for so it seemed good in Your sight. All things have been delivered to Me by My Father. Nor does anyone know the Father except the Son, and the one to whom the Son wills to reveal Him. Come to Me, all you who labor and are heavy laden, and I will give you rest. Take My yoke upon you and learn from Me, for I am gentle and lowly in heart, and you will find rest for your souls. For My yoke is easy and My burden is light." (Matthew 12:25-30)

One thing that I am–and that is a learner! I love to learn about people, about the Word of God and about how we think. As the scripture in Matthew 6:33 states we should first seek (through active listening and learning) the Kingdom of God (God's kingship) and His righteousness (living how the Word directs).

God shows us how to seek His Kingdom through His inspired Word, nature, and the universe. In seeking the Kingdom first, we all should recognize the Lordship of Jesus, God the Father, and our seal of redemption the Holy Spirit, for all things. Also, we should seek right relationship with God through reverential awe.

There may be times when learning something new can be a challenge. It is during this time that your relationship with and faith in the Lord will come into play. Learning how to learn can also be a challenge, but through discipline and obedience, all things are possible.

The process of learning how to learn is a four-fold process of (1) preparation, (2) exploration, (3) implementation, and (4) review.

1. Preparation: The preparation stage is the time for pausing to consider the goals and objectives you have set for yourself

and thinking ahead about how and when God is telling you to move. This is not the time for standing still, but the time for finalizing the plan that God has given you and analyzing each task of that plan. This is also the time of discovery and allowing God to reveal the various components of the journey; understanding what you will need to know and be able to do when the plan is accomplished, and the essential requirements of the task ahead.

2. Exploration: This is the phase where you seek the Word of God and search out the deep mysteries of His Word, while at the same time, developing a process for monitoring your progress. It is always a good plan to maintain a prayer journal with dates for each entry. The journal allows you to record your thoughts to God. It's possible to begin by writing down any thoughts to a passage of scripture you just read or write out the specific prayer you just prayed to God as though you were writing to a dear friend. Looking back and reflecting back on the inspired Word of God will be a great encouragement to keep you in the place of continuous pursuit of God with your whole heart and soul.

3. Implementation: This is the phase where you can monitor your progress and make a self-assessment. The immediate tasks required by God will now be completed. Implementation doesn't mean waiting until the end to determine your progress. This also involves checking during the time of actual work to determine whether you're on task, or if the Lord is making appropriate changes as you work. This is also the time to ask God for any clarification so that you will know how to use the gifts and talents He has given you to use.

Self-Assessment can be a critical skill to develop. It will help you to identify any gaps in what God has required of you and what you have actually been able to produce. Maintaining an optimistic outlook is also key. Remember, that every negative thought that you replay in your mind is like an anchor holding you back. Never give up; believe through faith that you can do all things through Christ. Try to find the positive in every situation. (The children of Israel were held back for 40 years because of their negativity.)

Thomas Edison once said, "Many of life's failures are people who did not realize how close they were to success when they gave up."

4. <u>Review:</u> The review phase takes place when a specific task that you have been given has been completed. If God has placed individuals in your life who are to be used as accountability partners or stakeholders in your journey, they will provide your with much-needed feedback and provide you with encouragement and advise during those time when the journey seems arduous.

Always be open to learn. In all things, seek God and His righteousness in all situations (even for lost things), and things will be given (added) to you! Secondly, learn to maintain a reverential awe for God. Once this occurs, you will find it increasingly easier to reach a new level of praise for the Lord.

When you come to the Lord in prayer, come seeking His Kingdom first, come as a child, on your knees and seek Him for help. It always works!! God's Word is always sure and true!!

Merchant Mentality and Managing Your Style

"Again, the kingdom of heaven is like a merchant seeking beautiful pearls, who, when he had found one pearl of great price, went and sold all that he had and bought it." (Matthew 13:45)

I just completed a series called "Every time I turn around, He keeps blessing me". During the series, we learned how to stir up the blessings of God through many means. We learned how to change our way of thinking about God's blessings and how to live in the flow where God's multiple blessings reside in the spiritual realm. Also, while this series was being taught, many people in the church received bonuses, extra gifts, gift cards, money, and other blessings, just to name a few. It was also a time of healing and deliverance in the church. It was absolutely amazing how God moved in our church in such an awesome way. We believed and applied biblical principles and saw much fruit.

There was a lovely lady in our church who gave me about 100 pairs of pearl earrings to give to the ladies in the church as a special "blessing" gift. She also volunteered to purchase the men of the church gifts of handkerchiefs with the initials "HKBM" (He Keeps Blessing Me) embroidered on them. We learned that the pearls symbolized the wisdom of God for us to make sound decisions in our daily lives.

The Kingdom of God is like a pearl of great price. We should hold onto the wisdom of the Word of God, at all costs. As merchants, we do not sell the Word of God, but we are to offer the Word to others who might not already know our Lord. We are ambassadors, God's representatives in this earth realm to minister to the lost and hurting.

We, in fact, are pearls of great price. We contain the wisdom of God to make a difference in this world. We should sell out for the Lord by giving up everything to Him, knowing that He will give us His everything.

"For this you know, that no fornicator, unclean person, nor covetous man, who is an idolater, has any inheritance in the kingdom of Christ and God. Let no one deceive you with empty words, for because of these things the wrath of God comes upon the sons of disobedience. Therefore do not be partakers with them." (Ephesians 5:5-7)

"I say than: Walk in the Spirit, and you shall not fulfill the lust of the flesh. For the flesh lusts against the Spirit, and the Spirit against the flesh; and these are contrary to one another; so that you do not do the things that you wish. But if you are led by the Spirit, you are not under the law. Now the works of the flesh are evident, which are adultery, fornication, uncleanness, lewdness, idolatry, sorcery, hatred, contentions, jealousies, outbursts of wrath, selfish ambitions, dissentions, heresies, envy, murders, drunkenness, revelries, and the like; of which I tell you beforehand, just as I told you in time past, that those who practice

such things will not inherit the kingdom of God." (Galatians 5:16-21)

"Do you not know that the unrighteous will not inherit the kingdom of God? Do not be deceived. Neither fornicators, nor idolaters, nor adulterers, nor homosexuals, or sodomites, not thieves, nor covetous, or drunkards, nor revilers, nor extortioners will inherit the kingdom of God." (1 Corinthians 6:9-10)

"Now this I say, brethren, that flesh and blood cannot inherit the kingdom of God; nor does corruption inherit incorruption." (1 Corinthians 15:50)

Caution: we will sometimes allow the flesh to get in the way of making wise decisions. Always walk away from anything that is counterfeit or contrary to the Word of God. When you walk in the Spirit, the Holy Spirit will guide you to a better way. Management of our lifestyle is paramount in the Kingdom of God. Our life has a style or sway (level of influence). What sway does your life have? Is your life governed by the ways of God or the ways of the world? Which voice do you listen to daily–Gods, the enemy, yours, or reason?

In a conversation with a friend, he mentioned that we should really watch our associations with others. If you hang out with people who are not following the Word of God, you could be influenced by them. Be careful in that regard. Either you are influencing them or they are influencing you! There is usually no middle ground. Time will tell who wins. The animal you feed wins. Manage your style by staying away from any suspicious activity.

"But the fruit of the Spirit is love, joy, peace, longsuffering, kindness, goodness, faithfulness, gentleness, self-control. Against such there is no law. And those who are Christ's have crucified the flesh with its passions and desires. If we live in the Spirit, let us also walk in the Spirit." (Galatians 5:22-25)

A tree is known by its fruit (Luke 6:44). What type of fruit do you bring forth? There is no law against the type of fruit from the Holy Spirit. You can produce, produce and produce it. In Christ Jesus, your flesh is put to death and the fruit of the Spirit lives forever more.

Commitment and Investment

"Then He said, 'To what shall we liken the kingdom of God? Or with what parable shall we picture it? It is like a mustard seed which, when it is sown on the ground, is smaller than all the seeds on earth; but when it is sown, it grows up and becomes greater than all herbs, and shoots out large branches, so that the birds of the air may nest under its shade.'" (Mark 4:30-32)

The question that should be asked is, how committed are you? What is your investment into the Kingdom of God? Are you all in, or are you partially in? Are you souled out? One good thing to know is that if you start with just a little faith, watered by the Word, your faith can grow to become greater than all herbs with branches for the birds to nest in the shade. A mustard seed is really small. Mature eyes may need magnifying glasses to see it. Thank God, you are not being judged by mature eyes when it comes to faith. Faith matters in the eyes of God, and Him alone.

Someone once said, "faith is like having a direct line to God. As the prayer of faith flows up, His power flows down. As a result, you are more than adequate for the challenge. Failure is never final, as long as your faith doesn't fail."

Faith, according to scripture, is needed to please God. So, I recommend the mustard seed to you as a good start. Faith is putting your trust in everything God says. It is absolute trust. According to Hebrews chapter eleven "Now" faith has substance in God's eyes. It is the substance for reaping and trusting. Faith is evidence of things not seen. Faith is required to get things in God's Kingdom. Faith is what is needed to receive salvation, healing and deliverance. Jesus paid the price on Calvary's cross and got up with all power in His hands. But it requires faith to receive salvation and the promises of

God. Faith pleases God. Whew, I am so glad God gave us all a measure of faith (Romans 12:3). In that measure must have been a seed.

So, now we know you are committed. What are you investing in the Kingdom of God? Are you using your time, talents and resources to build the Kingdom? If your answer is yes, then that is great!

Sometimes the commitment you make will benefit you immensely, and at other times someone else will benefit. In either case, the character of the Kingdom requires your commitment and investment in order to reap a benefit.

"For the kingdom of heaven is like a man traveling to a far country, who called his own servants and delivered his goods to them. And to one he gave five talents, to another two, and to another one, to each according to his own ability; and immediately he went on a journey. Then he who had received the five talents went and traded with them, and made another five talents. And likewise he who had received two gained two more also. But he who had received one went and dug in the ground, and hid his lord's money. After a long time the lord of those servants came and settled accounts with them. "So he who had received five talents came and brought five other talents, saying, 'Lord, you delivered to me five talents; look, I have gained five more talents besides them.' His lord said to him, 'Well done, good and faithful servant; you were faithful over a few things, I will make you ruler over many things. Enter into the joy of your lord. He also who had received two talents came and said, 'Lord, you delivered to me two talents; look, I have gained two more talents besides them.' His lord said to him, 'Well done, good and faithful servant; you have been faithful over a few things, I will make you ruler over many things. Enter into the joy of your lord.' "Then he who had received the one talent came and said, 'Lord, I knew you to be a hard man, reaping where you have not sown, and gathering where you have not scattered seed. And I was afraid, and went and hid your talent in the ground. Look, there you have what is yours.' "But his lord answered and said to him, 'You wicked and lazy servant, you knew that I reap where I have not sown, and gather where I have not

scattered seed. So you ought to have deposited my money with the bankers, and at my coming I would have received back my own with interest. So take the talent from him, and give it to him who has ten talents. 'For to everyone who has, more will be given, and he will have abundance; but from him who does not have, even what he has will be taken away.'" (Matthew 25:14-29)

God will give you the ability to live this life with a godly character. When God places you in an assignment, He will give you resources as a seed to do your assigned task and to bear fruit for His Kingdom. You may be very talented and have an abundance of resources. God expects us to use those talents to glorify Him and bear fruit for His Kingdom. Otherwise, you are wasting the precious gifts given to you by God. This parable is about money specifically, but can apply to your talents and gifts. God pours into us many gifts as His investment into us and expects us to work with what we have to glorify His Name. So, do not be afraid to use what God gave you to the best of your ability.

When I was young, I used to play the piano. I took lessons from a local teacher who was a pretty good musician and had lots of theory knowledge. I learned how to play songs from the greatest composers as a well as a few gospel songs here and there. I was not the greatest pianist, but I would try. Because I was not so great, I did not invest the time needed to be much better. On a weekly basis, I was required to play the piano for 30 minutes to an hour a day to prepare for my weekly lessons. I quickly learned that if I played the same song over and over again, I would get really good at that song.

That is what I did. I learned a few songs and was really good at them. I made the investment in certain favorite songs and perfected them. One thing I did not do was to stretch myself to learn more and get better at a variety of songs.

Will you commit to make an investment to stretch yourself and reach a deeper, richer place in Jesus? The choice is up to you. I believe that the great commission requires that of us–to go broad, wide and deep for the Lord.

"Then the kingdom of heaven shall be likened to ten virgins who took their lamps and went out to meet the bridegroom. Now five of them were wise, and five were foolish. Those who were foolish took their lamps and took no oil with them, but the wise took oil in their vessels with their lamps. But while the bridegroom was delayed, they all slumbered and slept. "And at midnight a cry was heard: 'Behold, the bridegroom is coming; go out to meet him!' Then all those virgins arose and trimmed their lamps. And the foolish said to the wise, 'Give us some of your oil, for our lamps are going out.' But the wise answered, saying, 'No, lest there should not be enough for us and you; but go rather to those who sell, and buy for yourselves.' And while they went to buy, the bridegroom came, and those who were ready went in with him to the wedding; and the door was shut. "Afterward the other virgins came also, saying, 'Lord, Lord, open to us!' But he answered and said, 'Assuredly, I say to you, I do not know you.' Watch therefore, for you know neither the day nor the hour in which the Son of Man is coming." (Matthew 25:1-13)

When we go broader, wider and deeper in the Lord, we will be ready for anything that comes. Later in my teens and early twenties, I was asked to play the piano for local churches. By learning the theory, I was able to read music and play most hymns and gospels. As the more contemporary works came along, it was a struggle for me to keep up with the choir. I practiced longer hours and stretched to meet the needs of the church. It worked out, but it would have been much better had I committed myself earlier in life and invested in wise actions.

Humility

"Assuredly, I say to you, unless you are converted and become as little children, you will by no means enter the kingdom of heaven. Therefore whoever humbles himself as this little child is the greatest in the kingdom of heaven. Whoever receives one little child like this in My name receives Me." (Matthew 18:3-5)

"But He gives more grace. Therefore He says: 'God resists the proud, but gives grace to the humble.'" (James 4:6)

Having a job working on the U. S. Space Shuttle was certainly an act of God's grace. I was in awe over the fact that God chose me to work there. I buckled down, and worked really hard to do a good job and got rewarded. I never thought the NASA assignment was God's stepping stone which would lead me to preaching and teaching the gospel. Humble yourself as a child–and you will be the greatest in the Kingdom of Heaven. Humble yourself, and God will bring you to do continued great things in His Name.

At one of Never the Same Ministries women's conferences, we learned about God's grace (unmerited favor). One of the speakers, Bishop Jackie Green, gave us all pink erasers and asked us to write the word "grace" on them. She reminded us that grace serves as an eraser in the spirit to rid and cleanse us of all our sin and unrighteousness. What great learning! I keep my eraser on my desk daily to remind me of His precious matchless grace.

As a citizen of the Kingdom of Christ, we are to follow and promote Him. Christ followed a path of humility, knowing that God would exalt Him. Are you displaying Kingdom humility in the people, places, and positions you seek? Are you content with taking out the trash at church, with serving instead of leading, or with being passed over for recognition by people–knowing that your stand is determined by God? The degree to which you have taking the character of the Kingdom to heart will be reflected in the places you seek and the one you promote.

Being humble is knowing who is resident Owner and Lord in our lives and bowing down to Him as King. God is always the Boss. Some of us have the wrong boss–we choose others and even ourselves over God. It is God who fuels us day to day. He ignites us and lifts us to higher heights to Him. Seek more grace by being humble and God will elevate you in due season.

Altitude Focused

"But God, who is rich in mercy, because of His great love with which He loved us, even when we were dead in trespasses, made us alive together with Christ (by grace you have been saved), and raised us up together, and made us sit together in the heavenly places in Christ Jesus, that in the ages to come He might show the exceeding riches of His grace in His kindness toward us in Christ Jesus." (Ephesians 2:4-7)

"You are the salt of the earth; but if the salt loses its flavor, how shall it be seasoned? It is then good for nothing but to be thrown out and trampled underfoot by men. You are the light of the world. A city that is set on a hill cannot be hidden. Nor do they light a lamp and put it under a basket, but on a lampstand, and it gives light to all who are in the house. Let your light so shine before men, that they may see your good works and glorify your Father in heaven." (Matthew 5:13-16)

God has placed us in heavenly places in Christ Jesus. This means that we should live our lives in a heavenly atmosphere, and our thinking should also reflect that fact. We are the body of Christ. Jesus is the head and we are His agents assigned on earth to effectively do His will.

I have flown in many airplanes over the years, and I have never seen one stay on the ground to reach its destination. They always took flight and went to a higher altitude, souring to its intended destination. There were times that we were stuck on the runway and sometimes circling in the air because the conditions were not favorable to take off or land; but we always ended up in the air.

According to wiki answers on the internet about height and speed of aircraft: "a typical altitude for a modern jetliner is anywhere from 24,000 feet to 39,000 above the ground. Commercial jets can cruise at 500 or 600 miles per hour. Some military jets can travel well over 7,600 miles per hour."

I learned four important elements about getting into the right altitude. Two key positive elements are speed to get the plane traveling fast enough, and lift to get the plane off the ground into the right altitude. There are two challenges to speed and lift–those challenges are weight and drag. Weight is easy to see and understand. An airplane weighs thousands of pounds without passengers, cargo and luggage. When we add people, pets and other things, the airplane can weigh a lot. Drag is what pulls the plane down and attempts to keep the plane from moving forward.

We sit in heavenly places and are able to be *lifted* above our situations and problems to a heavenly sphere with Christ Jesus as our Head. We can move at a *speed* and due season commensurate with our Savior's agenda. We are the salt of the earth. Nothing should *weigh* us down. We are to let our light shine before mean and not allow anyone or anything to become a *drag* in our daily lives.

Repent and Take Risks (for the Kingdom)

"Repent, for the kingdom of heaven is at hand!" (Matthew 3:2)

"From that time Jesus began to preach and to say, 'Repent, for the kingdom of heaven is at hand.'" (Matthew 4:17)

I am continually saying, "I apologize." There are times in my past that I really did not mean to do anything better or different, I just felt bad that I had hurt someone. Let me give you an example:

One day in my twenties, I was driving in my new car down the road. The posted speed limit was 35 mph, but I was driving well above the speed limit. I had internalized that it was okay to speed; I was doing the world a favor by getting to my destination quickly–which, of course, required me to speed. One day, I found myself pulled over on the side of the road with a blue light flashing in my rear view mirror. Well, you guessed it! I got a ticket for speeding. I gave my apology to the officer for speeding, but at that time, I had no intention to stop speeding forever.

Repentance is making a turn in different direction from the one you were heading that led to the wrong action. Apologizing is instance specific, and repentance requires an expected lifestyle change. Repentance is a matter of your heart and your intentions to never do a thing again. It means that you turn your back on that thing or action and expect to never do it again. Repentance is key in having a godly Kingdom character. Apologies are a good step toward the right direction. However, apologies do not necessarily speak to a lasting commitment from your heart.

John the Baptizer (Baptist) and Jesus the Christ both say that we should repent...the kingdom has come.

"And Mordecai told them to answer Esther: 'Do not think in your heart that you will escape in the king's palace any more than all the other Jews. For if you remain completely silent at this time, relief and deliverance will arise for the Jews from another place, but you and your father's house will perish. Yet who knows whether you have come to the kingdom for such a time as this?' Then Esther told them to reply to Mordecai: 'Go, gather all the Jews who are present in Shushan, and fast for me; neither eat nor drink for three days, night or day. My maids and I will fast likewise. And so I will go to the king, which is against the law; and if I perish, I perish!' So Mordecai went his way and did according to all that Esther commanded him." (Esther 4:13-17)

Taking a risk means that many times we should take a stand for something to build the Kingdom and possibly to save a life for the Kingdom. In Esther's case, she was saving a nation from imminent danger from a long-standing enemy, Hamon. Hamon stood for evil, and evil alone, against the nation of Israel. His intent was to annihilate the Jews from the face of the earth. Esther was asked by Mordecai (her relative who raised her as a child) to take a risk by going to the king uninvited to save the nation. It was unheard of for a person to go before a king uninvited. Esther took the risk and bowed before the king with her request for dinner (banquet), and she used this time to talk about the fate of her nation.

76

The king granted Esther's request and the nation was saved. Esther took a risk for her nation.

We should take risks for the Kingdom today. Integrity is needed today. Speak up for your brother or sister in the right way and time when they are being treated harshly. Speak up for Jesus with boldness.

Align (Strategically with Your Purpose)

"...who has saved us and called us with a holy calling, not according to our works, but according to His own purpose and grace which was given to us in Christ Jesus before time began."
(2 Timothy 1:9)

"...that is, that God was in Christ reconciling the world to Himself, not imputing their trespasses to them, and has committed to us the word of reconciliation. Now then, we are ambassadors for Christ,"
(2 Corinthians 5:19-20a)

I have had so many discussions these days about purpose and destiny. There are questions to be answered on the subject. Purpose is what God originally designed you to do. Destiny is reaching that place.

In October 2011, I will be taking a road trip to New Mexico with three other women. We are in the process of preparing for our trip. As we prepare, we have information on how far it will be to our destination from Tucson. The nearly 400-mile trip will require a lot of preparation. We will need to pack the right clothes (which will probably require a coat because we are going to a mountain retreat), money, reliable transportation, GPS/maps, and a secured place to stay when we arrive. Our purpose (intent) is to minister to the women about Christ, provide insights about walking in His divine will for their lives, and to give God glory at the retreat.

Our purpose is to preach and teach, and our destiny, of course, is New Mexico. Just like we need to prepare for our trip in advance, God has prepared us to do His original will for us to glorify Him. He mapped into us exactly what we needed to be successful in His eyes (obedience, right living, ordered steps, love of God, love of others and self...). Knowing that our ultimate destination is to be with the Lord in eternity, we also have a destiny here on earth.

Through prayer, God will reveal your purpose and destiny to you. You will be surprised what God as planned for your life. I am sure the Apostle Paul and our father of faith, Abraham were amazed at the impact their purpose had on so many lives.

In the final analysis, God calls us to be ministers of His gospel, to be committed to the Word of reconciliation, to follow Christ as His ambassadors, and to bear fruit that will remain for His Kingdom. Your purpose is to be in alignment with His Word and to make Him known. Your destiny will always lead to Christ. Your strategy should be to align yourself with the Word of God, pray, study, fast....and within time, your purposed destiny will emerge.

Cultivate Your Full Range

"But blessed are your eyes for they see, and your ears for they hear; for assuredly, I say to you that many prophets and righteous men desired to see what you see, and did not see it, and to hear what you hear, and did not hear it. "Therefore hear the parable of the sower: When anyone hears the word of the kingdom, and does not understand it, then the wicked one comes and snatches away what was sown in his heart. This is he who received seed by the wayside. But he who received the seed on stony places, this is he who hears the word and immediately receives it with joy; yet he has no root in himself, but endures only for a while. For when tribulation or persecution arises because of the word, immediately he stumbles. Now he who received seed among the thorns is he who hears the word, and the cares of this world and the deceitfulness of riches choke the word, and he becomes unfruitful. But he who received seed on the good ground is he who hears the word and understands it, who indeed bears fruit and produces: some a hundredfold, some sixty, some thirty." (Matthew 13:16-23)

"And He said, "To you it has been given to know the mysteries of the kingdom of God, but to the rest it is given in parables, that

"Seeing they may not see, and hearing they may not understand.""
(Luke 8:10)

"No longer do I call you servants, for a servant does not know what his master is doing; but I have called you friends, for all things that I heard from My Father I have made known to you. You did not choose Me, but I chose you and appointed you that you should go and bear fruit, and that your fruit should remain, that whatever you ask the Father in My name He may give you. These things I command you, that you love one another." (John 15:15-17)

I know a lady who had dream one day about a HUGE warehouse with many well-furnished rooms. She also lived in this warehouse. The warehouse had three levels, two of which she had explored and the third level is one that she did not know existed. The warehouse also had a place to park many vehicles and had a ramp for cars to drive upon.

Each of the rooms were already furnished and ready made to suit her tastes. When she was awakened from the dream, she wondered what it all meant. God spoke with her and provided an interpretation to her dream. What she believed she heard God say was that He had given her many rooms (ministries) to pursue, but she had not explored fully what He had given to her. In her heart, she believed God to say that she was off doing other things and was not pursuing what He had for her to do. Immediately, she began to seek God's will and agenda for her life in ministry. Within a few weeks she had started a couple of new ministries directed by the Holy Spirit.

To cultivate our full range, we should seek the Holy Spirit on a daily basis to reveal to us what is on God's mind for us. Developing your full range will cause you to leave your comfort zone and arc of safety to move in the anointing that God has placed in your care. When you develop you full range, you will see miracles, signs and wonders happen around you. When you develop your full range, you may be asked to move to another city, start new ministries, or venture out to do things you never imagined doing before.

Paul taught Timothy to develop his full range in preaching. He encouraged young Timothy to preach the Word no matter what–in season or out of season, when they wanted to hear him or not, when he was popular or unpopular, and even when he felt like it or did not feel like it.

Have you allowed God to develop your full range in your life? Are you up for the task no matter what? Are you ready to use your current skills for the Kingdom and develop other skills necessary to advance God's Kingdom? Don't pull back; it is part of your appointment to bear fruit for Christ–fruit that will remain. When God calls you to bear fruit by moving across country or to another part of the world, will you be ready?

Take Action Testimony

"And they overcame him by the blood of the Lamb and by the word of their testimony, and they did not love their lives to the death."
(Revelation 12:11)

I met a woman who told me the awesome story about the September 11, 2001, event where the World Trade Center towers in New York and the Pentagon in Washington, D.C. were stuck by terrorists. This event changed the lives of millions of Americans and people abroad for years.

She worked in the Pentagon, and as I remember the story being told, she routinely met a friend each day for coffee. One day, she was going to the elevator to meet her friend in the coffee shop and found that she did not have enough change to complete her purchase. She decided to go back to her office to get more money for the coffee. When she got back to her office, she felt the shaking and heard a rumble in the building where she worked. She thought that there must have been an earthquake in the city or something unusual had happened. Her first thought was to leave immediately and go get her young children from school because if there was something going on in the city, the schools would let out early and she did not want her children to have to wait for her.

She hailed a taxi and asked the driver to take her as quickly as possible to her children's school because there was an earthquake or something that just happened where she worked. She had no clue that an airplane with terrorists had deliberately run into the building where she worked and into the World Trade Center towers. The taxi driver told her what happened, and she was amazed that her life was spared. It took a few minutes for her to recover from what she heard. She was so overwhelmed by what she heard, she blacked out for a few minutes.

Finally, she reached her children's school and got home safely. She was thankful that God spared her life during this awful ordeal. She tells her story to many people as a testament of her faith in God. She tells people that God is an awesome God. He can take a situation like the one she faced and turn it around for His glory.

What about you? Your testimony may not be as profound as this ladies' testimony, but it could be just as impactful for God's Kingdom. You should take every opportunity to tell your stories to people as a witness to the goodness of God.

Your testimony may be just what a person desperately needs to hear in order to make a decision, to keep living, to meet an emotional need, or maybe just to encourage them to move forward.

Endure

"Therefore, having been justified by faith, we have peace with God through our Lord Jesus Christ, through whom also we have access by faith into this grace in which we stand, and rejoice in hope of the glory of God. And not only that, but we also glory in tribulations, knowing that tribulation produces perseverance; and perseverance, character; and character, hope. Now hope does not disappoint, because the love of God has been poured out in our hearts by the Holy Spirit who was given to us." (Romans 5:1-5)

"Yet in all these things we are more than conquerors through Him who loved us. For I am persuaded that neither death nor life, nor angels nor principalities nor powers, nor things present nor things to come, nor height nor depth, nor any other created thing, shall be

able to separate us from the love of God which is in Christ Jesus our Lord." (Romans 8:37-39)

"If we endure, we shall also reign with Him." (2 Timothy 2:12a)

Our world economy is going through so much unrest these days. So many people have been laid off their jobs, and finding employment continues to be a challenge for so many. As more than conquerors, we must stay strong and endure through these times and look for Jesus to bring us out.

One of my co-workers encourages me to endure through my new exercise regimen. When he sees me in the hall at work, he always asks how my exercise routine is going. His questions are quite probing to ensure that I am enduring the changes in lifestyle. One day he asked me how much weight I was lifting, how many repetitions I was doing in a set, and how many sets in each workout. I proceeded to answer his questions. As I was answering with a cheerful voice, he said, "Hmmmmm…Sounds to me like you are building a sprinter's body. No wonder you feel the way you do after your workout…"

I asked him to explain in layman's terms about what he meant. He asked me if I had ever noticed the difference between a sprinter's body and a marathon runner's body. I replied, "No." He continued to explain that a sprinter has strong thick muscles for heavy movement–especially in their legs. A marathon runner, on the other hand, has strong lean muscles for distance.

He further suggested that for me to endure, I should take the marathoner's course of action. His recommendation included less weight, more repetitions and more sets. He said that this would help me to be strong and endure. Endurance through more repetitions and more sets in life will build kingly character and enable you to endure.

What about you? While on this race, are you pacing yourself by lifting heavy weights without giving it all over to Jesus? Are you trying to lift it all yourself or are you allowing the yoke of the Lord to guide you? When you do it all yourself, you will be strong in the wrong way…and independent from God.

Be persuaded to endure.

Reach

I am a work in progress. How cool is that? It is God who made me and who will sustain me forever. He asks us to work together as a body to get the Kingdom mandate done. I believe working together encourages us to "Reach":

> Reach out to others that may provide innovative insights given by God to be helpful for your progress. Join a team of community Kingdom-minded people and work together with them to make things happen.
>
> Reach up to our Lord and Savior for witty inventions and creative ideas to advance the Kingdom. Also, God may assign godly leaders or authorities to help with His agenda.
>
> Reach in for introspection and a renewed mind daily as Romans 12:2 states. Reach in to ensure that you are engaged in a Kingdom mindset.
>
> Reach back and help others in their time of need. God will assign you to help others in your family, church, community, and nation and across the world.

6. Exercise Your Authority

Always know that there is nothing more powerful than the spoken word. A famous author named James Allen once wrote, *"A man sooner or later discovers that he is the master-gardener of his soul, the director of his life."* What that means to me is that I can choose to change my life and exercise the authority that God has already placed in me. We also know from the Word of God that anything we may be able to see was first made from that which is not seen.[1]

"By faith we understand that the worlds were framed by the word of God, so that the things which are seen were not made of things which are visible." (Hebrews 11:3)

This lets us know that anything that we are able to experience with our five senses was first brought forth from the spiritual realm and the manifest power of God. Moreover, this is the same power that rests in each of us. Furthermore, without a thing first being conceived in the mind and then being spoken out—without calling those things that are not as though they were (Romans 4:17)—nothing that currently exists would exist. This is not a mystical statement or an opinion. This is the principle of how the world was framed from the beginning, when God first created the heavens and the earth.

"And whatever you ask in My name, that I will do, that the Father may be glorified in the Son. If you ask anything in My name, I will do it." (John 14:13-14)

A major factor in exercising your authority is believing that you have the right to ask for what you want. All the necessary resources are already at your disposal. The presence of the Holy Spirit makes this evident, and praying and asking for what you want in Jesus' Name places His power and glory in the forefront.

Whenever you are in the holy presence of God and you have His full attention and blessing, there is nothing that the enemy can do to you; he has no access to you when you are in the presence of God.

"Then the seventy returned with joy, saying, 'Lord, even the demons are subject to us in Your name.' And He said to them, 'I saw Satan fall like lightning from heaven. Behold, I give you the authority to trample on serpents and scorpions, and over all the power of the enemy, and nothing shall by any means hurt you. Nevertheless do not rejoice in this, that the spirits are subject to you, but rather rejoice because your names are written in heaven.'" (Luke 10:17-19)

Prayer is essential to the exercise of authority. Through prayer you can make the most of every opportunity you are given. The walk of true holiness secures you as a vessel of honor and glory and prepares you for every good work for the Lord. The critical piece is in learning to harness, and then maximize, the potential of your thoughts and words.

You were created as a royal priest, and therefore, you have to be able to create a royal priestly mind-set by exercising noble thought habits and by disciplining your tongue to speak success-filled words in order to become the ambassador and champion that God made you to be.[2]

86

"You will also declare a thing, and it will be established for you; so light will be established on your ways." (Job 22:28)

Just as you can choose to change your life and exercise God's authority in your life, you can also choose to speak the right words. This scripture in Job confirms that the favor of God is poured out upon you because you belong to Him. This is similar to the anointing oil that was poured upon David by the prophet Samuel. It signified he was to be the next king of Israel. David was not initially given a crown; he was first anointed with oil–a symbol of the Holy Spirit and God's awesome approval and blessing.

The favor of God is extended through the walk of holiness and is evidenced by obedience because of the love you have for Christ Jesus. Loving Him and keeping His commandments comes with the assurance of enjoying the comfort from His Holy Spirit. That assurance comes with the blessings of a life with Him, union with Him, receiving His teachings and His peace, and being able to operate as His ambassadors.

Jesus Promises Another Helper

"If you love Me, keep My commandments. And I will pray the Father, and He will give you another Helper, that He may abide with you forever— the Spirit of truth, whom the world cannot receive, because it neither sees Him nor knows Him; but you know Him, for He dwells with you and will be in you. I will not leave you orphans; I will come to you." (John 14:15-18)

"And being assembled together with them, He commanded them not to depart from Jerusalem, but to wait for the Promise of the Father, 'which,' He said, 'you have heard from Me; for John truly baptized with water, but you shall be baptized with the Holy Spirit not many days from now.' But you shall receive power when the Holy Spirit has come upon you; and you shall be witnesses to Me." (Acts 1:4-5, 8)

The Holy Spirit is the source of strength and the power of God. This power and authority was conferred upon Jesus' Apostles, who were His direct and personal ambassadors. He also is a great Comforter who will never leave nor forsake you.[3]

1. He is a loving Comforter. No one has ever loved us the way He does (see Romans 5:5).
2. He is a faithful Comforter. He never fails and sin will never be able to separate us from His love. He loved us even when we were dead in sin (see Romans 15:3).
3. He is an untiring Comforter. He never loses heart, never gets tired, and never wearies–even by our sins, and not even by our stubborn refusal to accept His comfort (see John 14:26).
4. He is a wise Comforter. He correctly diagnoses all our problems, understands the causes of our diseases, finds the root of the problem, and is able to cure all of them, making us acceptable in the eyes of God (see 1 Corinthians 2:10).
5. He is a safe Comforter. He knows the heart and the will of God, and His comfort will never be contrary to them. Therefore, we can safely place all our trust in Him (see 1 Corinthians 2:13).
6. He is an active Comforter. He intercedes for us, reminding of us God's promises and His grace (see Romans 8:26-27).
7. He is an ever-present Comforter. He will never leave or forsake us. We do not have to send for Him–He is always right there (see John 14:16).

Indwelling of the Father and the Son

"A little while longer and the world will see Me no more, but you will see Me. Because I live, you will live also. At that day you will know that I am in My Father, and you in Me, and I in you. He who has My commandments and keeps them, it is he who loves Me. And he who loves Me will be loved by My Father, and I will love him and manifest Myself to him." Judas (not Iscariot) said to Him, "Lord, how is it that You will manifest Yourself to us, and not to the world?" Jesus answered and said to him, "If anyone loves Me, he will keep My word; and My Father will love him, and We will come to him and make Our home with him. He who does not love Me does not keep My words; and the word which you hear is not Mine but the Father's who sent Me." (John 14:19-24)

The Gift of His Peace

*"These things I have spoken to you while being present with you.
But the Helper, the Holy Spirit, whom the Father will send in My
name, He will teach you all things, and bring to your remembrance
all things that I said to you. Peace I leave with you, My peace I
give to you; not as the world gives do I give to you. Let not your
heart be troubled, neither let it be afraid. You have heard Me say
to you, 'I am going away and coming back to you.' If you loved
Me, you would rejoice because I said, 'I am going to the Father,'
for My Father is greater than I. "And now I have told you before it
comes, that when it does come to pass, you may believe. I will no
longer talk much with you, for the ruler of this world is coming,
and he has nothing in Me. But that the world may know that I love
the Father, and as the Father gave Me commandment, so I do.
Arise, let us go from here." (John 14:25-31)*

- There were more believers added daily as a result of the work of the Apostles and the acts of the Holy Spirit through them.
- Using the Name of Jesus carries weight (John 16:24; Matthew 28:18; John 14:12-14).
- This is the first recorded miracle that happened after the Holy Spirit came upon the disciples and gave them power.
- Miracles, signs and wonders followed the preaching and ministry of early church leaders–the early church readily accepted miracles, signs, and wonders.
- The early church prayed for miracles and seeing them was not random, occasional events, but as worthy evidences of God's anointing and continually glorifying Christ through the church.
- This recorded miracle gives the key for believers to exercise authority in faith.
- What God did through the believers in the early church, is available today.
- Leverage Kingdom power.

7. Leverage Kingdom Power

In order to be able to activate and leverage Kingdom power, you have to first be *in* and be a *part of* the Kingdom. And the only way to be in and also part of the Kingdom is through Jesus Christ. The threshold of the Kingdom is the cross of Christ.

Hebrews 1:3 tells us that God sustains *all* things by the Word of His power. Everything is controlled by His mighty hand. All He has to do is speak His will and then His power will accomplish it. For example, He formed the mountains by His power. He divided the seas by His power. He divided the light from the darkness by His power in Genesis 1:4. He created man by His power in Genesis 1:26. And He quickens the dead and calls them to life by His power in Romans 4:17.

> *"For He spoke, and it was done; He commanded, and it stood fast." (Psalm 33:9)*

He is the source of all power. Moreover, Romans 13:1 lets us know that *"there is no authority except from God, and the authorities that exist are appointed by God."* He places rulers in positions of power, and He controls our lives and our destinies by His power. A good example comes from the book of Genesis when we look at the lives of Abraham and his wife Sarah. God had promised them a son, but it was completely impossible for them to conceive. Yet, nothing is too hard for God. Something totally impossible was made possible by His power. Sarah did conceive and brought forth a son who later played a major role in God's plan for mankind.

What should be remembered is that if we place our faith in God, He promises each of us a portion of that same power. Through His power we have the ability to execute the impossible.

"But you shall receive power when the Holy Spirit has come upon you; and you shall be witnesses to Me in Jerusalem, and in all Judea and Samaria, and to the end of the earth." (Acts 1:8)

The purpose of God's power is to come alongside us, with the indwelling of His Holy Spirit, to help us to accomplish three (3) things:

1. Learn how to be sanctified (walk in holiness),
2. Learn how to partake of Christ's life, and
3. Learn how to become overcomers in order to bear righteous fruit.

The process of sanctification/holiness leads to partaking–partaking leads to overcoming–overcoming leads to inheritance. God's power not only gives us a new spirit when we are born again, but His power also produces a transformed life (see 1 Peter 1:5).

"But truly I am full of power by the Spirit of the LORD, And of justice and might, To declare to Jacob his transgression And to Israel his sin." (Micah 3:8)

A good example of the outworking of God's power is that of a young minister, who I will call Bob, who was born without any arms or legs. Although Bob is unable to walk and is confined to a wheelchair, this incredible young man has a wife and children, he is an awesome prayer warrior, and he travels extensively giving lectures, teaching, and ministering to large masses of people offering healing and deliverance. This extraordinary young man is not only born of the Spirit, but he also understands what it means to depend upon God's power for everything. Bob doesn't have any limbs, but he certainly is an example of one who walks in the Spirit and in the power of God.

"So he answered and said to me: "This is the word of the LORD to Zerubbabel: 'Not by might nor by power, but by My Spirit,' Says the LORD of hosts. 'Who are you, O great mountain? Before Zerubbabel you shall become a plain! And he shall bring forth the capstone With shouts of "Grace, grace to it!""" (Zechariah 4:6-7)

To be able to walk in and leverage Kingdom power, you should know exactly how it works in a believer. Before becoming a believer, God's Spirit of power works *with* us, leading and drawing us to Himself (see Acts 19:2). We become drawn to Him as He pursues us. After we respond with our personal invitation, God's Spirit comes *in* us and indwells us. This is when He unites our spirit with His and gives us a new heart and spirit. We are now born again and justified.

At the point when we are born again, God implants His eternal life (which includes His love, wisdom and power), into our hearts and we become the temple of His Holy Spirit. It is at this time that the Spirit comes *upon* us and empowers us. This is the baptism of the Holy Spirit (see Acts 1:8), and this is the time when God's power is to be used for the purpose of being genuine witnesses of Christ in our daily walk–not just in our words. Without this power indwelling us, we would be just like those having a form of godliness but denying the power within (see 2 Timothy 3:5).[1]

The indwelling and empowering of the Holy Spirit should happen at the same time, however, for many believers it occurs on two separate occasions–often many years apart–because they typically don't know enough to ask for the empowering.

93

"And whatever things you ask in prayer, believing, you will receive." (Matthew 21:22)

After we have been indwelt and empowered, it is critical to be refilled daily with the power of the Spirit from the inside out (see Ephesians 5:17-18). This filling means that we are to be continually filled and empowered, and not quench the Spirit. It now becomes our responsibility to choose to stay cleansed and sanctified. This is the true mark of holiness because it is not something that occurs automatically. It is God's will for us to be holy, but it is our choice as to whether or not we want to do it. We get to decide to make the right faith choices. God is the One who empowers us.

Individuals who experience this power will discover an explosive type of energy that will launch them further than anything they could have achieved on their own. Of course, this does not mean that you can be expected to be seen doing weird or spooky things. It simply means that the work that God has purposed in you through the gospel of Jesus Christ is now fully empowered and activated through you. You now have the power to do all things through Him.

This is why it is essential that we not stop our growth process at the step of salvation, thinking that this is good enough for our lives in Christ. Galatians 5:25 teaches us to not only live in the Spirit, but to also walk in the Spirit. It is the Spirit that brings us to Christ and then gives us His life. He then empowers us to be His reflection in everything we do.

Lastly, it is our job to stay cleansed, filled and empowered. The excellency of the power must be of God and not from ourselves. He promises us that in the end, He will raise us up by this same power; just as He did with Jesus Christ.

"But if the Spirit of Him who raised Jesus from the dead dwells in you, He who raised Christ from the dead will also give life to your mortal bodies through His Spirit who dwells in you." (Romans 8:11)

8. Make a Lasting Impact

Explore Your Strengths

We have learned what it takes to receive God's power and to be able to walk in it. However, in order to make a lasting spiritual impact upon your community, church, workplace, home, etc., it will be necessary to ask yourself some hard questions; in particular, what area(s) do you have the greatest potential? This is not the same as asking yourself things like: What do I like? What will make me the most money? What will make me happy in the short-term?

There are a myriad of things and areas to which that you can pursue and dedicate your life. They could even have the potential of earning you a decent living in the process. However, there are very few things wherein which you will have the opportunity to make a permanent mark.

"For You formed my inward parts; You covered me in my mother's womb. I will praise You, for I am fearfully and wonderfully made; Marvelous are Your works, And that my soul knows very well. My frame was not hidden from You, when I was made in secret, and skillfully wrought in the lowest parts of the earth. Your eyes saw my substance, being yet unformed. And in Your book they all were written, the days fashioned for me, when as yet there were none of them." (Psalm 139:13-16)

God's power is magnified in the development of human life before birth. So, even before you were born, God had a purpose and a design for your life, and His power and strength were inherently placed in you when life was breathed into you. Bringing this power and strength to the forefront and being able to make a lasting impact within your sphere of influence requires specific aim or intent on your part. In order to do that, some critical questions should have already been asked and answered.[1]

- What is my current position–where do I stand with God?
- What are the gifts and talents that I have to work with?
- Where do I desire them to take me?
- How do I get there from here?

The answer to the first two questions requires careful examination and consideration of your spiritual strengths and weaknesses and a determination of how to create the greatest impact utilizing those strengths.

"But God, who is rich in mercy, because of His great love with which He loved us, even when we were dead in trespasses, made us alive together with Christ (by grace you have been saved), and raised us up together, and made us sit together in the heavenly places in Christ Jesus, that in the ages to come He might show the exceeding riches of His grace in His kindness toward us in Christ Jesus. For by grace you have been saved through faith, and that not of yourselves; it is the gift of God." (Ephesians 2:4-8)

Whether you believe it or realize it or not, you are a holiness visionary. When God blessed you with gifts and talents, there was also a vision placed in you with a plan for activating those gifts and talents. The next step in answering the third question is articulating that holy vision and knowing who the person or persons are that exist in your life and will be instrumental in being a stakeholder(s) to assist in achieving your vision.

"Write the vision and make it plain on tablets, that he may run who reads it." (Habakkuk 2:2)

The last question involves articulating your spiritual goals and strategies for the purpose of achieving results. Your strategy should be a reflection of your strengths and weaknesses. For example, if you have to be able to conduct your ministry goals and take food to feed the homeless and you have a lack of transportation, you would need to identify what your weaknesses, and strengths, would be in that scenario and what you could do to overcome those weaknesses and build upon the strengths.

Make a Plan

The next step in being able to make a lasting impact is to formulate a plan. By now you have a good idea of what your gifts and strengths are and the areas wherein which you have the greatest influence. At that same time, you should have also been able to identify the areas where there may be potential growth areas.

Making a plan requires the ability to somehow measure your progress; to make a determination of what will be your key performance indicators (KPIs). The measurement of your progress can be accomplished by:

- Defining your objectives and understanding the nature of what you are doing (what God has purposed you to do), knowing what will be accomplished, and knowing what is the measurement of your success.
- Determining how that success is to be measured; and should there be any struggles or failures along the way, how they are to be overcome.
- Establishing checkpoints (allowing for personal reflection and correction) to determine if your goals are being achieved or if the plan requires some modification(s).
- Daily prayer and meditation on the Word to acquire direction and information. Through prayer, God will reveal how you are progressing and will advise if there should be any changes to the plan.

97

Take Action

"Therefore, my beloved, as you have always obeyed, not as in my presence only, but now much more in my absence, work out your own salvation with fear and trembling; for it is God who works in you both to will and to do for His good pleasure." (Philippians 2:12-13)

Now that you have a plan, it's time to take action. The expectation in today's culture is that there will be immediate success and that things will begin to happen instantly. However, the reality is that many may not experience their greatest work until some years of consistent effort have been invested. The same is true for the work of holiness in our lives. Sanctification and holiness is a continuous process of consecration and dedication.

"For a righteous man may fall seven times and rise again, but the wicked shall fall by calamity." (Proverbs 24:16)

Holiness is not only what God gives us, but it is what we *manifest* that God has given us. If this were not so, then He would receive no glory from our lives. Until we show the world that something different is available, then they will function in the same way that they have always functioned.

Remember that a fall is not necessarily a failure. The greatest hindrance to holiness is disobedience to the Word and the known will of God. The Lord is not a brute, nor is He rude and overbearing. If you refuse to do as He instructs, you will probably not be struck by a lightening bolt, but He will gently withdraw from you and let you do as you choose.

An example of God's incredible grace and mercy is seen in the relationship He had with David (read 2 Samuel). David was a man after God's own heart and he was single-mindedly committed to God, yet he was guilty of some serious sins. His life was a roller coaster of emotional highs and lows, but his strengths included enormous courage in battle and unfailing trust and faith in God for protection.

The lessons we learn from David include the following:

- Honest self-examination is necessary to recognize your own sin and then be able to repent of it. We may try to fool ourselves, but we can never hide our sin from God.
- God always offers forgiveness of our sins, but we cannot escape the consequences.
- God highly values our faith in Him. Despite any of life's ups and downs, God is always present to give us comfort and help.

David's action plan included a constant desire to be in the presence of God. And because of his faith and hunger for God, the Lord rewarded him by making an everlasting covenant with him to keep his house in the lineage of the throne and pointed him to Jesus. The plan of holiness does come with eternal rewards.

Celebrate Progress

General Colin Powell once said, "*Success is the result of perfection, hard work, learning from failure, loyalty and persistence.*" Hard work always produces results. When you experience progress in the walk of holiness, do not be afraid to take time to celebrate that success. Both small and big wins deserve time for recognition and reflection.

It is hard to stay motivated if too much time goes by without making any progress. If while on the journey of holiness it appears that no progress is being made, then it may be a signal that a change of course is necessary. Progress will keep you moving forward, and understanding what leads to that success will allow you to continue to repeat it. Do not be so focused on your next goal or project that you miss the opportunity to recognize the mile markers along the way.

Recognize Your Influence

"But you are a chosen generation, a royal priesthood, a holy nation, His own special people, that you may proclaim the praises of Him who called you out of darkness into His marvelous light."
(1 Peter 2:9)

Recognizing your influence is not a precursor to pride and boastfulness. Your walk and assurance of who you are in Christ puts you in a position of influence. God personally selected you for this position, and it is a position that not only serves a mighty and majestic King, it is one that exercises rule.

Your royal priesthood position actually allows you to spiritually hold two offices; first, as a king, and secondly as a priest of God. Jesus reigns as both King and Priest, and it is His will that His disciples should in many things become as He is. Just as Christ is the heir of God, so He lives; and it is His will that we live also. And just as Christ is in heaven in glory and it was His good pleasure to select you, so it is His will that we should be there with Him. Therefore, because He is both King and Priest, true believers are also kings and priests.

"Just as He chose us in Him before the foundation of the world, that we should be holy and without blame before Him in love, having predestined us to adoption as sons by Jesus Christ to Himself, according to the good pleasure of His will, to the praise of the glory of His grace, by which He made us accepted in the Beloved." (Ephesians 1:4-6)

Your function as a royal priest differs from that of your walk as an ambassador for Christ. As you walk in holiness as a priest, you represent yourself before God (who is invisible); but your walk as an ambassador for Christ means that you represent God before others (visible).

100

Your effective representation of God requires that there be a maturing relationship with Him; that's where the walk of holiness comes into play. As you mature in holiness through your walk with Him and He affects you in a positive way, you have the opportunity to effect change in others. How you use your influence is crucial. It will be a daily commitment to look for opportunities to use that influence in positive ways–on your job, at school, in the community, at church, etc.

Jesus required His disciples to literally be a front-line militia and impact the world. This did not require them living in isolation and separated from the world. Holiness requires being set apart, but not living in your own personal private kingdom. God's purpose in you has a social agenda and an outward expression of His principles. You are called to make a difference by influencing and impacting the world around you.

"You are the salt of the earth, but if the salt loses its flavor, how shall it be seasoned? It is then good for nothing but to be thrown out and trampled underfoot by men. You are the light of the world. A city that is set on a hill cannot be hidden. Nor do they light a lamp and put in under a basket, but on a lampstand, and it gives light to all who are in the house. Let your light so shine before men, that they may see your good works and glorify your Father in heaven." (Matthew 5:13-16)

The one way to influence and make a lasting impact on the world around you is by becoming being salt and light. It may appear to some that the church, in many areas, has lost its influence in the community. The reason may be because it has neglected its responsibility of being salt and light. As we have neglected to be what God has called us to be, then the world, in direct response, has decided to ignore us. When we are salt and light, the world will listen; and when we are not, then they won't. Salt is a preservative, a flavoring, an antiseptic, and it creates thirst. Light dispels darkness, it reveals, awakens, and gives warning of danger.

Your influence is to be salt and light. Your salt seasoning brings out the God-flavors of His earth, and your light illuminates and releases the God-colors to the world around you. If you lose your saltiness, then people will not be able to taste of His goodness. God is not a secret that has to be kept. By releasing that light to others, they will then be prompted to open up to God.

The sphere of your influence is the world. Just as salt differs from pepper and light differs from darkness, so you are distinct from the world. Your distinction makes a difference in the world. In the world of advertising, it's called positioning. In the world of sports, it's called strategy. In the Christian walk, that difference is called holiness.

It is possible to lose your saltiness and light. One way for salt to lose its flavor is to become diluted when mixed with something else. It's dangerously easy for believers to become diluted and lose their preserving influence in the world. Dilution is prevented with daily exposure to Jesus, spending time in His Word, and soaking up his light rays through prayer.

A weekly contact with God produces a weak influence. A daily contact with God produces a dynamic influence.

9. Align Your Kingdom Compass

"My brethren, count it all joy when you fall into various trials, knowing that the testing of your faith produces patience. But let patience have its perfect work, that you may be perfect and complete, lacking nothing. If any of you lacks wisdom, let him ask of God, who gives to all liberally and without reproach, and it will be given to him. But let him ask in faith, with no doubting, for he who doubts is like a wave of the sea driven and tossed by the wind. For let not that man suppose that he will receive anything from the Lord; he is a double-minded man, unstable in all his ways. Let the lowly brother glory in his exaltation, but the rich in his humiliation, because as a flower of the field he will pass away. For no sooner has the sun risen with a burning heat than it withers the grass; its flower falls, and its beautiful appearance perishes. So the rich man also will fad away in his pursuits. Blessed is the man who endures temptation; for when he has been approved, he will receive the crown of life which the Lord has promised to those who love Him." (James 1:2-12)

Our Kingdom compass is the direct and true alignment with the order of God. It is in this place that we fulfill His mission and what He has purposed in us. When we are in that true alignment, we are aligned with power, potential, and lasting energy, and we are connected to the targets that God has already established for us.

Even during times of temptation, we have God's assurance that our endurance through it all guarantees the crown of life to those who truly love Him.

When we consider the purpose of a compass in the physical sense, we should understand that it is a device used to determine geographical direction and is usually mounted with a freely pivoting magnetic needle that aligns itself the magnetic field of the earth. In order to align yourself to the compass, you first must establish the angle of magnetic north and true north. Your magnetic north is determined by the earth's magnetic field and usually points toward the North Pole. However, true north is the direction in which you point yourself in order to reach the North Pole.

When going on a long hike or journey in an unfamiliar area, it's a good idea to take along a compass. In an open country where there is clear visibility or when looking above the natural treeline, finding routes may come as easy as looking for specific landmarks. But if you happen to be in a densely wooded area or forest where there is low visibility, a compass is needed to stay oriented.

If, while you are on your journey, you happen upon some particular obstacle and are deflected off course, then the compass is useful in getting you back on track. All that is needed is to note the compass bearing of the direction you are walking in, then count your steps or the time you spent off course. After skirting the obstacle, return to your original course with the same number of steps or timing. Once you are aligned, you are now able to resume your primary heading.

Many new cars are equipped with directional devices called a GPS (global positioning system). There are some people who think that they have an internal compass and natural sense of direction and will ignore the GPS direction. This usually results in becoming lost and ultimately being forced to use the GPS device and recalibrate their position in order to reach their intended destination.

Your spiritual compass operates much the same way. The directional devise you need to keep you on track is the workings of the Holy Spirit. Keeping yourself aligned in the Kingdom requires listening to the Lord and obedience to His leading. When we make a wrong turn or are guilty of trying to direct ourselves believing we know a better route, and later find ourselves in a lost place, the Holy Spirit will prompt you and guide you into going the right direction.

Our reasons for choosing our own directions vary, but often times it is because of the uncertainty in not knowing where a particular road will lead, and at other times we may be having difficulties in making sense of the road that the Lord has us on. It is at this time that we begin to question things. Why is this road so bumpy? Shouldn't it be smoothly paved? Don't I deserve a nice easy ride?

There will be times when you come to a fork in the road and will need to know the direction that God has for you. The road may even be filled with pitfalls and obstacles, littered with potholes, or there may be roadblocks and detours because the road is "under construction."

"I will instruct you and teach you in the way you should go; I will guide you with My eye." *(Psalm 32:8)*

When that happens, you will need to be able to hear God's voice and take heed to His spiritual GPS (God's Positioning System).[1] There are a few steps needed to keep yourself aligned with a Kingdom compass. Those steps include the following:

- Ask for wisdom (see Proverbs 2:1-7). You need God's direction in every area of your life. How you respond to His leading will dictate how you reflect Christ daily. That response may be needed on your hectic job, when there is chaos at home with the children, and even when you are flipping through television channels and a show catches your eye that may be destructive to your soul.

"However, when He, the Spirit of truth, has come, He will guide you into all truth; for He will not speak on His own authority, but whatever He hears He will speak; and He will tell you things to come." *(John 16:13)*

105

- Once you receive God's wisdom, commit to following it. James describes a person who asks for wisdom then chooses to go in his own direction as being like waves tossed in the ocean.

"Therefore do not be unwise, but understand what the will of the Lord is." (Ephesians 5:17)

Consider this example: On the windward side of the island of Oahu, there is a tiny island with a cove having steep cliffs on each side. Waves come in from all directions and bounce off the cliffs in all directions. It may seem fun to jump off the cliff and into the cove, but when you land in the water, it's extremely difficult to navigate and swim out. You may start out in one direction, but a few seconds later, you will find yourself going in the opposite direction. There are sharp rocks all around and at times there may even be hungry sharks circling on the bottom.

If you find yourself doubting God's ability or willingness to give you the wisdom you need, then James describes you as being like waves that are being tossed by the wind; restless, moving back and forth in all directions, and unable to be settled.

- Make plans in humility. Setting both short- and long-term plans for yourself is to be commended. God gave everyone free will. The key is to follow His Word and truly rely on the wisdom we receive from the Holy Spirit as we do.
- Live your life with dependence. Because we have been given free will, we have the ability to select what career to pursue, who to marry, where to live, how many children to have, where to send them to school, etc. However, we should always remember that God's sovereign will is the ultimate authority. Any plan that we can come up with will only be successful if He wills that it be so. A key point to remember is that not everything in this Christian walk will be smooth. If your godly plan, which was made in humble dependence upon God, ultimately fails, the lesson to be learned is that of patience.

"Now these things became our examples, to the intent that we should not lust after evil things as they also lusted. And do not become idolaters as were some of them. As it is written, 'The people sat down to eat and drink, and rose up to play." Nor let us commit sexual immorality, as some of them did, and in one day twenty-three thousand fell; nor let us tempt Christ, as some of them also tempted, and were destroyed by serpents; nor complain, as some of them also complained, and were destroyed by the destroyer. Now all these things happened to them as examples, and they were written for our admonition, upon whom the ends of the ages have come. Therefore let him who thinks he stands take heed lest he fall. No temptation has overtaken you except such as is common to man; but God is faithful, who will not allow you to be tempted beyond what you are able, but with the temptation will also make the way of escape, that you may be able to bear it." (Ephesians 10:6-13)

"All things are lawful for me, but not all things are helpful; all things are lawful for me, but not all things edify. Let no one seek his own, but each one the other's well-being."
(Ephesians 10:23-24)

- Endure trying times with patience. You may not know God's ultimate plan, but you can know His daily guidance. Job's life was a perfect example. No one in the bible suffered like Job. When the Holy Spirit's guidance appears to lead you into a test, then you know you are in good company because Jesus is our best example of God's greater purpose.

Following God's guidance does not mean that life will be easier. Most assuredly it almost always means that life will be more rewarding and we will share times of strengthening. But the promise of Christ is that He will guide us, empower us, and even carry us through those trying times.

10. Achieve Spiritual Position

"Now therefore, if you will indeed obey My voice and keep My covenant, then you shall be a special treasure to Me above all people; for all the earth is Mine. And you shall be to Me a kingdom of priests and a holy nation." (Exodus 19:5-6)

"Therefore, my beloved brethren, be steadfast, immovable, always abounding in the work of the Lord, knowing that your labor is not in vain in the Lord." (1 Corinthians 15:58)

To all those who walk in holiness, are obedient to the Word of God, and who keep His covenants, He promises to bestow upon you a special position and allow you to represent Him in the earth realm as His representative. The position you receive is that of being a special treasure, a kingdom of priests, and a holy nation.[1]

Just as God distinguished the people of Israel from all other nations, He also distinguishes true followers of Christ. You are a chosen generation. You are also a royal priesthood, a holy nation, a peculiar people, agreeable to what was spoken of in Exodus 19:5-6. God knew you, delivered you from bondage of sin, and then He shapes you into what He wants you to be.

"The Lord delighted only in your fathers, to love them, and He chose to love; and He chose their descendants after them, you above all peoples, as it is this day." (Deuteronomy 10:15)

There was also a promise made to Israel; that if they were obedient to the Lord, they would be made a kingdom of priests. Here we are said to be a priesthood of kings, or a royal priesthood.

True followers of Christ are chosen generation and are chosen for two reasons:

1. They are chosen by God, out of everyone else in the world, to be His.
2. God's people are of a peculiar descent and/or pedigree. You have an excellent ancestry and are different from all the rest of the world.

"They shall be Mine, says the LORD of hosts, on the day that I make them My jewels. And I will spare them as a man spares his own son who serves him." (Malachi 3:17)

"For the LORD, has chosen Jacob for Himself, Israel for His special treasure." (Psalm 135:4)

Although you have an excellent ancestry, you were not chosen because you are an excellent person; but He chose you only for His good pleasure. By virtue of His choosing you, you have been made excellent. You were not first holy and then He chose you; but He chose you first, that you might be holy. Your selection by God did not come as a result of the good works you did prior to becoming saved. On the contrary; the good works you do now are because He chose you.

"You did not choose Me, but I chose you and appointed you that you should go and bear fruit, and that your fruit should remain,

110

that whatever you ask the Father in My name He may give you."
(John 15:16)

The fruit of a tree is the evidence of its being attached to the True Vine (see John 15:1-2), and the fruit of your life in Christ is regarded as holiness and sanctification as evidenced by Romans 6:22.

"...For everyone to whom much is given, from him much will be required; and to whom much has been committed, of him they will ask the more." (Luke 12:48)

The purpose of choosing you was for you to achieve a position of holiness, and by virtue of your achievement, others will be drawn to the Lord as well. Jesus is the true Vine and all who are true believers are the branches. He expects much fruit from His branches. He is not satisfied with little, but requires that the fruit be commensurate to His investment (read the parable about the talents in Matthew 25:14-30).

Those who walk in darkness are spoken of as being unfruitful (see Ephesians 5:11 and Romans 6:21), and those living an unregenerated life will produce fruit as unto death (see Galatians 5:19-20). However, it is very clear that the privilege of you being chosen by God did not rest on merit. He chose you simply because He loves you. It was His sovereign choice to make, and He made it with you in mind.

"For whom He foreknew, He also predestined to be conformed to the image of His Son, that He might be the firstborn among many brethren. Moreover whom He predestined, these He also called; whom He called, these He also justified; and whom He justified, these He also glorified." (Romans 8:29-30)

The goal of God's predestined purpose is to transform you into the image of His Son Jesus. This is the prize of the upward calling. The fact that God predestined and knew you before you were born, not only speaks to His omniscience, but it also speaks to the fact that your position in Him is no accident.

He knew you would be in this place, in this position, and at this time. He singly and distinctly set His love upon you and you have been favored among the rest of mankind.[2] Just as the high priests of the Old Testament bore the names of the twelve tribes of Israel upon their breastplates, Jesus, who is our High Priest, bears your name upon His heart and as a symbol of His devotion, you have been engraved in the palm of His hand.

"See, I have inscribed you on the palms of My hands; your walls are continually before Me." (Isaiah 49:16)

The position that you hold in Christ is in heavenly places. Begin to see yourself in that position and meditate on it. Start to see yourself as Jesus sees you. You are no longer a sinner saved by grace. You *were* a sinner, but now you are saved by grace.

Your mind has to become transformed to this because as a man thinks in his heart, so is he (see Proverbs 20:7). You are the sum total of your thoughts. Whatever is your deepest driving desire, so is your inspiration and your will; and as your will is, so are your deeds and so is your destiny. If you believe you are a sinner, then you will probably sin. However, if you see yourself as the righteousness in Christ Jesus, then you will act in righteousness.

The poet Johann Gottfried Von Herder was quoted as saying, *"Without inspiration the best powers of the mind remain dormant; there is a fuel within us which needs to be ignited with sparks."* Your thoughts are spiritual and so is the process of inspiration. What you believe can be accomplished starts with a concept in your mind. Your will is then joined with the intellect of your imagination; and then expectation sees it through.

In Chapter 11 of Genesis, the people thought that they could build a tower to heaven; and because they saw this tower in their minds, they were able to build it. God stopped them by confusing them and changing their language because the tower became an idol and their symbol of worship.

Start believing what God has already said in His Word about you (just to name a few):

- You are more than a conqueror.
- You are the first and not the last.
- You are the head and not the tail.
- You are above and not beneath.
- You are the beloved of God and seated in heavenly places.
- You are part of a royal priesthood.
- You are member of a chosen generation.
- You are an ambassador for Christ and light of the world.
- You are the salt of earth.
- You are fearfully and wonderfully made.
- You are the temple of the Holy Spirit.
- You are the bride of Christ.

"Jesus answered and said to him, 'Blessed are you, Simon Bar-Jonah, for flesh and blood has not revealed this to you, but My Father who is in heaven. And I also say to you that you are Peter, and on this rock I will build My church, and the gates of Hades shall not prevail against it. And I will give you the keys to the kingdom of heaven, and whatever you bind on earth will be bound in heaven, and whatever you loose on earth will be loosed in heaven'." (Matthew 16:17-19)

You were purposely built and designed for success. By virtue of your divine inheritance, Jesus has already equipped you to walk in your spiritual position, and as a true follower of Christ, you have already achieved it. You were given authority to rule and have dominion. The only thing left to do is to take your position and start walking it. Start decreeing and declaring the good news of the gospel of Jesus to the world. There are still many who don't know that He came to pay the price that they might have an abundant life.

113

11. Switch to a Pace of Excellence

There is a distinct difference between walking in excellence and walking in perfection.[1] A wikipedia psychological definition of perfectionism states that perfectionism is a personality trait characterized by a person striving for flawlessness and setting excessively high performance standards, accompanied by overly critical self-evaluations and concerns regarding others' evaluations.[2] Moreover, that same source states that excellence is a talent or quality which is unusually good and so surpasses ordinary standards.[3]

It is clear to see that one should strive more to be excellent than to be a perfectionist. The perfectionist is excessively concerned with self-evaluation, and as a result, is one who may be overly critical of him/herself and/or others. The person walking in excellence need not doubt nor be overly critical of goals and achievements; s/he simply possesses the quality of being outstanding or extremely good.

The individual walking a pace of excellence understands and is able to fully operate in their place of purpose. That person possesses the quality of being outstanding and has no problem doing what the Lord has called him/her to do and does it with wisdom and vigor.

"Finally, brethren, whatever things are true, whatever things are noble, whatever things are just, whatever things are pure, whatever things are lovely, whatever things are of good report, if there is any

virtue (excellence) *and if there is anything praiseworthy—meditate on these things." (Philippians 4:8)*

The perfection often spoken of in the Word is always perfection founded in Christ Jesus. The walk of holiness and sanctification encourages us in Matthew 5:48 to be perfect, just as our Father in heaven is perfect. Jesus sets an unattainable standard, and yet, even though that standard is impossible to meet, God cannot lower His standard without compromising His own perfection.

Perfectionism[2], therefore, refuses to accept anything other than perfection, which is based on our own strength. Human perfectionism usually results from a desire to control the tiniest of details, because something else exists in our lives that is chaotic and is most likely going wrong causing us to want to have some type of control over something. The perfectionist insists there is no margin for error, and as a direct result, places him/herself in the forefront because they generally do not understand how anything could possibly work other than if they are doing it. What generally happens is that it now becomes all about him or her, rather than about God.

"Now it happened as they went that He entered a certain village; and a certain woman named Martha welcomed Him into her house. And she had a sister called Mary, who also sat at Jesus' feet and heart His word. But Martha was distracted with much serving, and she approached Him and said, 'Lord, do You not care that my sister has left me to serve alone? Therefore tell her to help me'. And Jesus answered and said to her, 'Martha, Martha, you are worried and troubled about many things. But one thing is needed, and Mary has chosen that good part, which will not be taken away from her'." (Luke 10:38-42)

Martha's need to make certain that everything was perfect placed her in a position where she was distracted and in anxious. She was so busy fussing with the details of the evening, which Jesus obviously thought were unnecessary, that she missed the most important thing;

being in the Lord's presence, worshiping Him, and listening to His Words.

In order to establish a pace of excellence, there are some things and some motives that should be examined on a daily basis:

- What is it that you are doing that will ultimately bring glory to God, and not to yourself?
- Are your actions in line with God's plan for your life?
- How much time are you spending with the Lord, and is there a balance between work and rest?
- Are you choosing to take control of the things that belong in His hands?

The book of Daniel provides an superb example of one who walked with a pace of excellence. He was an individual who possessed a great deal of influence; even with the king. He had experience, wisdom, leadership skills, ability, and a reputation that was above reproach. The king was so impressed with Daniel, that he proposed to elevate him to a position over the whole realm. This was not something that the other leaders took kindly to; and because of their jealousy, they plotted to set a trap for Daniel in order to get rid of him.

"It pleased Darius to set over the kingdom one hundred and twenty satraps, to be over the whole kingdom; and over these, three governors, of whom Daniel was one, that the satraps might give account to them, so that the king would suffer no loss. Then this Daniel distinguished himself above the governors and satraps, because an excellent spirit was in him; and the king gave thought to setting him over the whole realm. So the governors and satraps sought to find some charge against Daniel concerning the kingdom; but they could find no charge or fault, because he was faithful; nor was there any error or fault found in him. Then these men said, 'We shall not find any charge against this Daniel unless we find it against him concerning the law of his God." (Daniel 6:1-5)

But Daniel was blameless before God. His relationship with God and his faith-filled excellent spirit provided a means of deliverance for him. The mouths of the lions were shut, and the king was relieved that Daniel was delivered. When he realized that Daniel's faith in God was at such an excellent level, he was pleased that Daniel's life was spared. He then commanded that those who wrongfully accused Daniel be tossed into the lion's den. In fact, he was so impressed with Daniel's God and how He delivered Daniel, that he made a decree that this God was God, and that His Kingdom is one that will never be destroyed, and that His dominion would endure forever.

Clearly, God honors those who honor Him. Daniel's pace of excellence was established through his strong faith and his unrelenting devotion to God. It did not matter to Daniel that there were people who were jealous of his gifts and who wanted him to be out of the picture. He refused to bow down to worship idol gods, and he continued to do as he had always done; he knelt down, and in front of an open window, facing Jerusalem, thanked God and prayed three times every day.

Everything Daniel did was done in excellence, and it was done without murmuring and complaining.

12. Create Spiritual Consonance

Whenever there is about to be a serious move of God and He is getting ready to do something powerful and tremendous, it is often preceded with a sound.

"When the Day of Pentecost had fully come, they were all with one accord in one place. And suddenly there came a sound from heaven, as of a rushing mighty wind, and it filled the whole house where they were sitting. Then there appeared to them divided tongues, as of fire, and one sat upon each of them. And they were all filled with the Holy Spirit and began to speak with other tongues, as the Spirit gave them utterance." (Acts 2 1:4)
"And the LORD said to Moses, 'Behold, I come to you in the thick cloud, that the people may hear when I speak with you, and believe you forever.' ...Then it came to pass on the third day, in the morning, that there were thunderings and lightnings, and a thick cloud on the mountain; and the sound of the trumpet was very loud, so that all the people who were in the camp trembled. And Moses brought the people out of the camp to meet with God, and they stood at the foot of the mountain. Now Mount Sinai was completely in smoke, because the LORD descended upon it in fire. Its smoke ascended like the smoke of a furnace, and the whole mountain quaked greatly. And when the blast of the trumpet sounded long and became louder and louder, Moses spoke, and God answered him by voice." (Exodus 19:9, 16-19)

Having a spiritual consonance (a harmony of sounds, rhythmic agreement) requires the ability to make a connection to the people. Moses connected to the people through His assignment from God. The next powerful occurrence was God's gift of the Ten Commandments. After centuries of being in Egyptian bondage, this was legislation needed for living properly as the people of God. The Law also distinguished them from other nations.

"For what great nation is there that has God so near to it, as the LORD our God is to us, for whatever reason we may call upon Him? And what great nation is there that has such statutes and righteous judgments as are in all this law which I set before you this day?" (Deuteronomy 4:7-8)

Being in harmony and spiritual consonance[1] is demonstrated through the power that the Lord has given you through prayer, faith, and obedience and it will be manifested through spiritual giftings.

Spiritual Gifts

"But to each one of us grace was given according to the measure of Christ's gift. ...And He Himself gave some to be apostles, some prophets, some evangelists, and some pastors and teachers, for the equipping of the saints for the work of ministry, for the edifying of the body of Christ, till we all come to the unity of the faith and of the knowledge of the Son of God, to a perfect man, to the measure of the stature of the fullness of Christ; that we should no longer be children, tossed to and fro and carried about with every wind of doctrine, by the trickery of men, in the cunning craftiness of deceitful plotting, but, speaking the truth in love, may grow up in all things into Him who is the head—Christ—from whom the whole body, joined and knit together by what every joint supplies, according to the effective working by which every part does its share, causes growth of the body for the edifying of itself in love." (Ephesians 4:7, 11-16)

120

Your spiritual gift is not something you find in pretty wrapping paper and tied with a fancy ribbon placed under a tree.[2] It also is not something that you can pick and choose as you wish. You do not get to pre-select your gift; but you do get to 'unwrap' it and use it. Your spiritual gift is an assignment from God, who gives you the ability, capacity and desire to perform a function within the body of Christ. Along with this awesome gift, He also gives you the supernatural energy, joy and effectiveness to carry out that function; and He provides divine inspiration to give you the ability to exercise the gift.

Diversity of gifts exist so that the body of Christ will function with order and with perfection. Just as God has sovereignly designed the physical body with many members, each functioning with a particular ability and for a specific purpose, so is true for the spiritual body in terms of diversity of gifts. (For example, the right foot does not have the capacity to perform the same function as the left shoulder.)

Every believer is born with a variety of talents and gifts, along with the divinely inspired spiritual gift(s). The service that each provides involves God the Father, the Son, and the Holy Spirit.

- The gifts of the Holy Spirit are the sovereign choice of the Holy Spirit.
- The place of our service is chosen by the Son of God.
- The workings and style of the ministry is determined by the Father.

"There are differences of ministries, but the same Lord. And there are diversities of activities, but it is the same God who works all in all. But the manifestation of the Spirit is given to each one for the profit of all." (1 Corinthians 12:5-7)

The New Man

"This I say, therefore, and testify in the Lord, that you should no longer walk as the rest of the Gentiles walk, in the futility of their mind, having their understanding darkened, being alienated from

121

*the life of God, because of the ignorance that is in them, because of
the blindness of their heart; who, being past feeling, have given
themselves over to lewdness, to work all uncleanness with
greediness. But you have not so learned Christ, if indeed you have
heard Him and have been taught by Him, as the truth is in Jesus:
that you put off, concerning your former conduct, the old man
which grows corrupt according to the deceitful lusts, and be
renewed in the spirit of your mind, and that you put on the new
man which was created according to God, in true righteousness
and holiness." (Ephesians 4:17-24)*

*"I beseech you therefore, brethren, by the mercies of God, that you
present your bodies a living sacrifice, holy, acceptable to God,
which is your reasonable service. And do not be conformed to this
world, but be transformed by the renewing of your mind, that you
may prove what is that good and acceptable and perfect will of
God." (Romans 12:1-2)*

At the point where holiness has become a true lifestyle–Your domain
space has been realized, you have developed and deployed Kingdom
action steps and leveraged Kingdom power and authority, and have
begun to walk in spiritual excellence–the 'new man' is reflected in
your daily walk and the former ungodly characteristics have been
forsaken.   You willingly turn away from the carnal and
unregenerated life. Your mind is now transformed and, as a direct
result, so is your thinking and your lifestyle.

- Futility of the mind no longer exists.
    - You willingly submit your mind to Christ and to God's
      thoughts instead of the world's way of thinking.
    - Your mind is renewed daily by the reading of the Word
    - You no longer depend on your own human reasoning
      because your mind is renewed daily by meditating and
      focusing on the Word.
    - You have deliberately committed to changing your
      thinking by bringing your thoughts in line with the Word
    - You consciously exercise positive thinking–you choose
      higher thoughts.
- You are not alienated from the life of God.

- o You are no longer estranged from all that is honest and good.
- o You are no longer spiritually separated from God because of ignorance to God's truth.
- o You are no longer in a state of utter spiritual ignorance where desperate wickedness prevails.
- ▪ Past feelings are behind you.
  - o You are no longer morally insensitive or apathetic to the consequences of sin.
- ▪ Lewdness and uncleanness are not a part of your life.
  - o You no longer allow yourself to succumb to sensuality.
  - o You have an awareness of the deceptiveness in thinking that there will be no consequence to a continued lifestyle of sin.

You are now in the place where your body has been presented to God as a living sacrifice. You are holy and acceptable because your life has been *completely* offered to the Lord. You have yielded yourself to God as a true instrument of righteousness.

Do Not Grieve the Spirit

"Therefore, putting away lying, 'Let each one of you speak truth with his neighbor,' for we are members of one another. 'Be angry, and do not sin': do not let the sun go down on your wrath, nor give place to the devil. Let him who stole steal no longer, but rather let him labor, working with his hands what is good, that he may have something to give him who has need. Let no corrupt word proceed out of your mouth, but what is good for necessary edification, that it may impart grace to the hearers. And do not grieve the Holy Spirit of God, by whom you were sealed for the day of redemption. Let all bitterness, wrath, anger, clamor, and evil speaking be put away from you, with all malice. And be kind to one another, tenderhearted, forgiving one another, even as God in Christ forgave you." (Ephesians 4:25-32)

When there is disharmony with the Spirit, a lack of spiritual consonance, the Spirit of God will be grieved. The existence of true love between two individuals means that they love each other and that they would want the best for each other. You would never deliberately hurt that person who truly loves you. This is how the Spirit feels about each true believer.

Upon first entering the Kingdom, we are to become one with Christ. Many new believers seek the 'comfort' of the church because there is a need to satisfy a longing in their spirit, or because they have become dissatisfied in some regard with life. They come looking for something better; something more meaningful and satisfying.

Upon discovering the true and living God, there is suddenly a challenge to walk in holiness and continue in a lifestyle of continuous sanctification. However, there is also now a tug-of-war in their spirit because of the temptation to fall back into the carnal lifestyle to which they were so accustomed.

The oneness and harmony of being completely in Christ is realized when it becomes painful for you to deliberately sin against God. The Spirit of God is grieved whenever we choose to sin against Him and follow our own worldly desires; when we choose to go against the One who truly loves us by loving our former lives more.

The grieving of the Spirit occurs when you feel that tug-of-war because you are pulling in one direction and the Spirit is trying to take you in the opposite direction. The result of this continued resistance is you will eventually begin to feel guilty about the choices you are making, and the things that satisfied you before coming to Christ will no longer satisfy you. Pretty soon your joy and energy may diminish and could be eventually replaced with listlessness and lethargy.

"When I kept silent, my bones grew old through my groaning all the day long. For day and night Your hand was heavy upon me; my vitality was turned into the drought of summer."
(Psalm 32:3-4)

The clear choice is to put away the bad choices of the flesh and live faithfully for the Lord. The correct road to follow is that road leading you closer to God and holiness, and therefore, farther away from the world of sin.

Unity through Humility

"Therefore if there is any consolation in Christ, if any comfort of love, if any fellowship of the Spirit, if any affection and mercy, fulfill my joy by being like-minded, having the same love, being of one accord, of one mind. Let nothing be done through selfish ambition or conceit, but in lowliness of mind let each esteem others better than himself. Let each of you look out not only for his own interests, but also for the interests of others." (Philippians 2:1-4)

The Holy Spirit desires to be in harmony and unity with you. This unity is similar to being in a partnership with Him. With that partnership comes the fulfillment of joy because now you are in union with Him, you have become like-minded, you share the same love, you are in one accord with Him, and you are now of one mind. The switch to holiness is complete with your desire to be in total union with the Holy Spirit of God.

Conclusion

"Finally, brethren, whatever things are true, whatever things are noble, whatever things are just, whatever things are pure, whatever things are lovely, whatever things are of good report, if there is any virtue and if there is anything praiseworthy—meditate on these things. The things which you learned and received and heard and saw in me, these do, and the God of peace will be with you. ...I can do all things through Christ who strengthens me." (Philippians 4:8-9, 13)

It is my desire for us all to keep the switch on. I trust this book has served as a great resource to you in getting to that place in the Lord. The goal of this book was also to provide you with valuable insights into how to switch from a place of beginning to a place of fullness in Christ.

Now that you have switched to holiness you will find yourself making the decision to serve better in your place of purpose to make a difference for God's kingdom. People who make the switch are convinced of the power and position that holiness carries. They understand that they have spiritual authority, and they recognize the importance and influence that the Name of Jesus Christ carries. Jesus has all authority over heaven and earth. He delegated authority to His followers and co-laborers to finish His work on earth and in the spiritual realm.

The power to carry out our all our assignments are done through the Holy Spirit. Holiness gives us the ability to be who God created us to be and to live a life far above expectations to a place of peace and authority to make disciples through the Name of Jesus. Holiness sets us apart for service and community.

The choice of holiness means we have fully stepped into the Kingdom of God and we fully trust Him for every moment of every day of our lives. Jesus gave His life for us, and now we can do no less than the same for Him. We have become one with Jesus and the transition between living according to the dictates of our sinful flesh and living according to the leading of the Holy Spirit has been completed.

We live a life of excellence. We celebrate Christ daily.

Our mission is completed, and we have remained true to ourselves and to our Lord. We have stepped into a space where nothing but Christ matters. We think only on the things of God.

We have now switched!!

WORKS CITED

1: Assess Your Domain Space
P. 13. Dictionary.com: Domain definition (accessed October 6, 2013).

2: Identify Your Current Spiritual Reality
P. 25. Florence Littauer "Personality Plus: How to Understand Others by Understanding Yourself"pp23-72 © 1992.

3: Implement Reverse Planning
P. 32. Standing for the Truth: Standingfortruth. wordpress.com. "Legalism versus Spiritual Discipline / Standing for Truth" (accessed October 6, 2013).

P. 34. Dr. Johnson C. Philip. "Carnality: Symptoms and Cure". November 19, 2008.

4: Develop and Deploy Kingdom Action
P. 40. Elizabeth Peale Allen. "Walking the Path of Holiness. Guideposts". Pawling, New York. http://www.guideposts.org/faith/bible-resources/walking-the-path-of-holiness, (accessed October 4, 2013).

P. 42. www.seekfind.net/HowCanIBeFreeofSinand WalkinTotalHoliness (accessed September 10, 2013).

6: Exercise Your Authority
P. 82. N. Cindy Trimm. "Commanding Your Morning— Unleash the Power of God In Your Life". Charisma House, 2007. Lake Mary, Florida.

P. 83. http://mb-soft.com/believe/txw/bibleaut.htm (accessed October 6, 2013).

P. 84. "Seven Attributes of the Holy Spirit". www.heavenawaits.com (accessed May, 2012)

7: Leverage Kingdom Power

P. 89. Nancy Missler. "God's Supernatural Power". "Koinonia" House 2012. http://www.khouse.org/articles /2012/1051 (accessed September 10, 2013)

8: Make a Lasting Impact

P. 92. Stan Simonton. "Lesson 7—Royal Priesthood and Royal Ambassadorship". www.Lessons. katycommunitychurch.org (accessed September 10, 2013)

9: Align Your Kingdom Compass

P. 101. Michele McLean. "Daily Devotion -- God's Positioning System". http://www.cbn.com/ spirituallife/devotions/mclean (accessed September 10, 2013).

10: Achieve Spiritual Position

P. 104. Jonathan Edwards. "Christians a Chosen Generation, a Royal Priesthood, a Holy Nation, a Peculiar People". (1703-1758). http://biblebb.com/ files/edwards/chosen.htm (accessed September 20,2013)

P. 106. Thy Way Ministries. "Comprehensive Bible Study– Our Spiritual Position". http://www.thy-way.org /Bibles_Studies (accessed September 20, 2013).

11: Switch to a Pace of Spiritual Excellence

P. 109. Words of Williams. "Walking in Excellence, Not Perfectionism". http://wordsofwilliams.com (accessed September 5, 2013).

P. 110. Wikipedia. http://en.wikipedia.org /wiki/Perfectionism_(psychology) "perfectionism" (accessed September 20, 2013)

12: Create Spiritual Consonance

P. 114. Dictionary.com, http://dictionary. reference.com/browse/consonance "consonance" (accessed September 11, 2013)

P. 114. Lambert Dolphin. "Description of the Spiritual Gifts". http://www.ldolphin.org/Spgifts.html (accessed September 20, 2013)

BIBLIOGRAPHY

Exhaustive Concordance of the Bible. Lahabra, CA: The Lockman Foundation -- Foundation Publications, Inc. Anaheim, CA; 1981, 1998.

The Spirit Filled Bible NKJV. Nelson Publishing, 2002.

Charles Stanley, *In Touch Magazine. 'The Greatest Act of Love' pg 36.*

New American Standard Bible, Updated Edition, 1995.

About the Author:

Dr. Amanda H. Goodson

Amanda is a native of Decatur, Alabama and currently resides in Tucson, Arizona where God has entrusted her to serve as Pastor. She also plans and facilitates seminars, workshops, and retreats for churches.

She is President and on the Board of Directors for Never the Same Ministries (NTS), a God inspired, Tucson based, Kingdom led ministry dedicated to serve as a vessel through which people are provided tools and resources to develop a more spiritually mature and improved relationship with God through Christ. The NTS God ordered mission is to provide biblically based instruction, tools and coaching for people within the community through planning and deployment of conferences and events across the United States.

God has gifted Amanda to be a Spirit-led preacher, teacher, trainer and coach for churches, agencies and non-profit organizations. Amanda connects with her audiences by sharing the Word of God through real-life experiences. She gives God glory as He allows her to inspire others to learn more about being a Spirit-led Christian in the world today. God has blessed her with an enthusiastic, energized and interactive method.

As a Kingdom citizen, she is fully submitted to the will of God. Her prayer is to be active in sharing her faith, to make her thoughts agreeable to the will of God, and to have the mind of Christ. The Word of God is the final authority in her life.

For further information or to book Dr. Goodson please contact her at:

AmandaGoodson.com

Books by Dr. Amanda Goodson

Spiritual Quickbooks^{TM}
Kingdom Character
Spiritual Authority
Carmel Voices
The Power to Make an Impact
Powerful People Follow Christ
Step out in Faith
Going Higher, Declarations for Kids
On the Rise
Spiritual Intelligence

Leadership Minibooks^{TM}
The Authority of a Leader
Character of a Leader
Unlock Your Full Potential
12 Power Principles for Administrative Professionals
Soar to Your Destiny

Leadership Workbooks
Unlock Your Full Potential Workbook

Cover design by Noah Paul

www.ingramcontent.com/pod-product-compliance
Lightning Source LLC
LaVergne TN
LVHW011245080426
835509LV00005B/640